MODERN JAPANESE FICTION

868–1926

AKAMURA Mitsuo

JAPANESE LIFE AND CULTURE SERIES

文学

KUSAI BUNKA SHINKOKAI

MODERN
JAPANESE FICTION
1868-1926

by NAKAMURA Mitsuo

KOKUSAI BUNKA SHINKOKAI

(Japan Cultural Society)

Tokyo, 1968

First edition, 1966 (Part One), 1968 (Part Two)
Revised edition, 1968

Published by KOKUSAI BUNKA SHINKOKAI, 55, 1-chome, Shiba Shirokane-dai-machi, Minato-ku, Tokyo, Japan. Distributed by JAPAN PUBLICATIONS TRADING COMPANY, Central P.O. Box 722, Tokyo; 1255 Howard Street, San Francisco, California 94103; 175 Fifth Avenue, New York, New York 10010. Copyright © 1966, 1968, by Kokusai Bunka Shinkokai; all rights reserved. Printed in Japan

LCC Card No. 68-58248

CONTENTS

PUBLISHER'S FOREWORD

It has long been regretted that students and scholars who engage in Japanese studies have to face many difficulties, not only in having to master a difficult language, but also in the matter of the lack of effective assistance by the learned institutions and people of this country. Recognizing this fact, the Kokusai Bunka Shinkokai (Japan Cultural Society), since shortly after its establishment in 1934, has been applying its energies to several programs for providing such facilities for foreign students and friends of Japan.

Initially the Society made a collection of Western-language books and magazines relating to Japan, which are available for reference at the K.B.S. Library, and published a full catalogue of the items collected during the years 1935–62, *A Classified List of Books in Western Languages Relating to Japan,* which is obtainable from the University of Tokyo Press.

Concurrently, since 1959 the Society has been compiling a series of bibliographies, under the series title *A Bibliography of Standard Reference Books for Japanese Studies with Descriptive Notes,* listing and describing the more important books written on Japan in Japanese. This is proving another valuable contribution to Japanese studies. Volumes already published cover the following fields: Generalia, Geography and Travel, History and Biography, Religion, History of Thought, Education, Language, Literature, Arts and Crafts, Theatre-Dance-Music, Manners and Customs and Folklore. In preparation are volumes covering: Politics, Law, and Economy.

Since 1961 the Society has also been publishing a series of books on

Japanese life and culture, including the present publication, which give basic guidance in introductory fields of Japanese studies. Out of more than fifteen such published studies, the Society has now selected a number, as listed on the first page of this volume, which have been revised and reissued. More volumes, both revisions and original editions, will appear successively. It is the sincere hope of the Society that this series, as well as its other activities, may prove of value to all who are interested in the study of Japan.

The author of the present work, Mr. NAKAMURA Mitsuo, is presently a professor of literature at Meiji University, Tokyo. As a critic, dramatist, and novelist, he has played a leading role in various fields of Japanese literary activity. His two Japanese-language works, *Modern Novel of Japan* (Iwanami, Tokyo, 1954, rev. 1964) and *History of Meiji Literature* (Chikuma, Tokyo, 1963), are remarkable contributions, giving a general survey of Japanese literary activity during the past hundred years. He is especially noted for his research on FUTABATEI Shimei, a writer of modern Japan's period of enlightenment. He has written several studies on the lives and works of FUTABATEI, TANIZAKI Jun'ichiro, SHIGA Naoya, and SATO Haruo, as well as a study of the novel of manners.

The book was originally published in two separate volumes entitled *Japanese Fiction in the Meiji Era* and *Japanese Fiction in the Taishô Era,* and the pagination of the original publications has here been retained, with each part beginning from page 1.

Our acknowledgments are due to the author for furnishing the text and selecting the illustrations, to Mr. Donald L. Philippi for translating Part I, to Mr. FUJIMURA Eiichi for translating Part II, and to Mr. David Griffith for editing the latter translation.

Two editorial notes: 1) The Hepburn system, with minor modifications, has been followed in romanizing Japanese words. 2) Japanese personal names are given in the Japanese style, family name first.

September, 1968   KOKUSAI BUNKA SHINKOKAI

PART ONE

JAPANESE FICTION IN THE MEIJI ERA

(1868-1912)

GINZA STREET, TOKYO IN THE EARLY MEIJI ERA
(depicted by one of the woodprint artists)

Before beginning our brief survey of the modern Japanese novel, let us consider the significance of modern Japanese fiction for us today.

The study of the novel has occupied the chief position in the history of Japanese literature of the Meiji and Taisho periods. This concentration on fiction would appear to have few parallels in the history of the modern literatures of other countries. In a sense, it may indicate a certain propensity on the part of today's literary historians. While even third-rate novelists of the Meiji and Taisho periods are being unearthed and made much of, at the same time in the fields of poetry, the drama and literary criticism that many writers and works which exerted far-reaching influences on their contemporaries is being unjustly neglected.

Nevertheless, this is not a tendency which the literary historians themselves have deliberately created. There must have been something in the Meiji-Taisho literature itself which led to the general acceptance of this fiction-centered view of literature.

Let us put it this way. Concisely, the novel is the least deceptive and the most reliable mirror of the spirit and the lives of the Meiji and post-Meiji Japanese.

The naturalistic movement in Japanese literature which came into existence toward the end of the Meiji period regarded the depiction of truth as the purpose of the novel. Literary naturalism, as is well known, finally came to confuse facts with truth. This line of thinking, however, did not spring into being suddenly together with naturalism. It may be said to have been one of the currents underlying all of Meiji literature from its very origins. This may also be one reason why Japanese naturalistic literature, while being strongly affected by European influences, still evolved through its own unique patterns.

"Eschew falsehood, forget ostentation, and behold acutely the realities of thine own situation. Having beheld, then confess them earnestly."

These words of Shimamura Hôgetsu were not merely a slogan expressing the tenets of naturalism. They were a declaration expressing a definite characteristic pervading the entire Meiji literature.

The Meiji period was a time when the patterns of living and thought of the populace underwent far-reaching changes under Western influences. Partly as a result of the very nature of Western civilization itself, these Western influences affected chiefly the more utilitarian aspects of life. Although this utilitarianism was more pronounced at the beginning, in general it remained unchanged throughout the Meiji and Taisho periods and on into the Showa period.

During these periods, literature, like the other branches of art—or perhaps even more than they—tended to be pushed aside into a corner by society as a "useless pursuit." Far from receiving governmental encouragement, it was much more often an object of suppression and disciplinary supervision. Literature grew up as something exclusively unofficial, sometimes even in the role of a sort of outcast kept deliberately in obscurity.

"Far be it from me, at this late date, to commence to wax indignant at the relationship between the state and art in the nation to which I belong. Quarreling with my parents and rebelling against my preceptors, I chose of my own free will the state of a poet, a vocation which the state never required of me—a vocation which it rather seeks to suppress violently. In choosing this state of my own accord, how could I fail to be prepared for all the inevitable consequences? . . . Poets are truly poisonous, evil weeds which the state seeks to eradicate with the sickle of its laws and regulations. It is nevertheless unable to eradicate completely these weeds, which continue to grow with each rain . . . 'Traitors worse than gamblers,' 'treacherous vagrants'—these are the titles of honor which we shall have to stomach forever."

These words of Nagai Kafū, although replete with the hyperbole for which he was renowned, do express vividly the position to which literature was relegated in those days.

From its very inceptions, Meiji literature occupied the position of a critic of contemporary social life. The various distinctive features of Meiji literature can be derived from this basic fact.

First of all, let us start from the more negative aspects. For one thing, this meant that the literary man was not taken seriously by society. According to the "sound" common sense of the period, the man of literature was regarded as a sort of failure. In actual fact, an interesting point of similarity between Narushima Ryūhoku and Kasai Zenzô was the fact that both of them liked to think of themselves as occupying the position of outlaws.

One of the distinctive features of Meiji literature was precisely this. In the midst of a society which held literature in light esteem, the Meiji writers, fired with their new sense of mission, were proud to endure poverty and the neglect of society. This gave to the Meiji novel a purity which has seldom been paralleled in other countries and in other periods. On the other hand, if one attempts to regard this as an expression of the Meiji *Zeitgeist,* it is undeniable that it is for this very reason quite narrow and one-sided. As we shall see later, this tendency becomes more and more pronounced as time goes on.

This same situation, however, also has its positive aspects. The very fact that they were ignored and left alone by society allowed the writers to create their own closed world, where they were free to indulge in artistic experiments and to live according to their new ethical standards, far removed from the customs inherited from the epoch of feudalism. As a result, the novelists of the Meiji and Taisho periods—particularly after naturalism—while on the one hand paying the price of estrangement from society, were on the other hand eager to keep in step with the most advanced ideas of the contemporary world; they staked their very lives on their desire to create art in this manner. A special society of their own, the *bundan* or literary world, was necessary in order to make possible this idealistic life attitude, that is, to make it possible for the writer to keep his head always full of the very latest ideas abroad in the world at large, while living himself in the society of an island kingdom in the Far East—and in a very secluded corner of that society, indeed.

Whether for good or for ill, the distinguishing characteristic of the modern Japanese novel is the fact that it developed in a manner quite removed from the context of the surrounding environment. This applies not only to the novel or to literature alone, but is characteristic of everything which has ever gone by the name of "culture" from the Meiji period until our own day. The history of the novel is of particular interest to us precisely because in it we can see this tragicomedy enacted with the most typical gestures.

Exactly as in all other fields of our modern culture, the Japanese novel has up to the present day followed a path of development which may be characterized as a process in which its points of weakness have been gradually unveiled in their most striking and undisguised form. The confusion which has arisen from this process now stands revealed before our eyes.

However, even when viewed thus with reference to the present situation, it is obvious that the modern Japanese novel does occupy a special position as distinguished from the other arts.

There is one distinctive feature which is obvious to all, not only in literature, but in other fields of Japanese art today. This feature is the coexistence of products of the native tradition and modern forms created under Western influence.

Obviously enough, in painting we have both Japanese style painting as well as Western style painting. In music, native Japanese music and Western music are both cultivated at the same time. Some such divisions are also present in literature. For instance, the field of drama is divided into the Kabuki drama and the "new" Shingeki (and one might also add the Shimpa drama as an intermediate form). In poetry, there is a clear contrast between the traditional *tanka* and *haiku* on the one hand and the modern poetry which originated under Western influence on the other.

Naturally, as long as these divergent forms exist in the same period and in the same society, it is unthinkable that they should be entirely without influence on each other. Thus, there are music lovers who say that they like both *nagauta* and violin music. Similarly, we know of many cases of Japanese style painters who have been influenced by Western painting and of composers of Western music who have incorporated Japanese melodies in their works. However, in spite of all this, it is a fact that in the realms of music and painting, both schools continue to rely upon entirely different raw materials and techniques and to adhere to quite different value systems.

In the field of poetry also, it would be easy to discover the penetration of Western literary concepts in today's *tanka* and *haiku,* while one can clearly discern traditional poetic notions in the works of many writers of "modern poetry."

Nevertheless, the *tanka* and *haiku* poets never write modern poetry, nor do the modern poets ever seriously write *tanka* or *haiku* as their literary output.

This phenomenon of coexistence of the classical arts with contemporary arts is no doubt present in every country in the world. However, there is probably no parallel anywhere for this situation, where two sets of such radically divergent art forms both survive with such vitality and continue to confront each other so profoundly in every field. In fact, this situation may be said to be the essential feature characterizing contemporary Japanese culture. The only strange thing about this is that the novel is the only field where this coexistence or dichotomy is completely missing.

Of course, contemporary Japanese novels are written on the basis of Western literary concepts. In fact, even the Japanese word for novel came to be used in its present sense as a result of the influence of modern Western novels. However, when we seek a Japanese counterpart for the novel,

just as we do when we contrast native Japanese music or Japanese painting with Western style music or painting, we must admit that at the
present time such a counterpart can no longer be found.

The popular literature called *taishû-bungaku,* particularly those tales
dealing with historical subjects, is in a certain sense a revival of the *gesaku*
tradition of the Edo period. At the time when this popular literature first
came into existence, it did indeed possess marked characteristics of the
older tradition, but today even it has become westernized in its contents.
In contemporary popular novels, even the historical personages experience no emotions which could not be explained in terms of the common-
sense experience of the contemporary Japanese. In other words, these
novels are set in the past but are peopled with Japanese exposed to Western influence in the same way as the contemporary Japanese. Thus, rather
than symbolizing a revival of tradition, these historical novels reveal instead that tradition has been lost to the contemporary Japanese, even in
the guise of history.

Reviewing the history of the Japanese novel since the Meiji period, we
observe that traditional elements comparable to Japanese music or Japanese painting retain their vitality in it until about the time of the Kenyûsha. In chronological terms, this corresponds to the period just before
the Russo-Japanese War.

The success of naturalism signified the triumph, both in style and in
contents, of literary concepts transplanted from the West over traditional
Japanese "art." In his novel *Shinkichôshano nikki* (Diary of a Person Recently
Returned from Abroad), Nagai Kafû has one of the characters remark:
"Purely Japanese literature died out completely around the year 1897.
The literature written after then is not Japanese literature. It is Western
literature written in the Japanese language for the sake of form only."
This is an interesting observation, particularly since Kafû himself was
opposed to the naturalistic movement of those times.

The naturalistic movement in literary circles soon went into a decline,
at least superficially, and was succeeded by various anti-naturalistic
schools, which, however, inherited unchanged all the basic features of
the revolution achieved by naturalism. Thus, the writers of the so-called

Tanbi-ha, of the Shirakaba-ha, and of the Shin-richi-ha all turned out work suiting their individual personalities but based on the groundwork built up by naturalism.

Shôsetsu Shinzui (The Essence of the Novel) by Tsubouchi Shôyô was the first serious attempt to transplant the modern Western concept of the novel. If naturalism represented a more or less successful realization of this concept in actual works of literature, then the "modernity" possessed by the writer, albeit in an idealistic manner, reached a point from which it could never retreat. In this way, the "modernity" formed under Western influence solely in the novel succeeded in annihilating the artistic concepts of the past and in replacing them completely. This inevitably led to a very special pattern of development of the Japanese novel.

When we think about the modern Japanese novel, we discover why the novel came to occupy this very special position in literature and, in a wider sense, among the arts in general. We also observe the abuses which resulted and the potentialities which were present in the novel.

The chief abuses may be said to be the following two. First, there was the formation of a special literary pseudo-society, the so-called *bundan*, which became particularly pronounced from the end of the Meiji period and during the Taisho period. The second was the novel's growing associalization, resulting from the idealistic nature of the "modernity" existed only in the writer's own mind.

Thus, the Japanese writer lived in a laboratory-like environment divorced from real society. However, as I mentioned before, as long as this environment really satisfied a need in the development of literature, it was the scene of serious, life-and-death struggles for the writers living in it. By separating themselves from society, these writers criticized their society.

For them, the novel was not merely an artistic representation of human life. Rather, it was a means of searching for a new, true way of living. At the same time, it was the record of this search.

This was the hazardous quest for the sake of which the writers of the Meiji and Taisho periods risked tragedy in their real lives. They had high,

probably exaggerated expectations of the novel, and they dared to believe in them and to *live* them.

For them, art was a path of mental and spiritual training, and the
search for truth meant living without pretense. This ethical passion made
these people, eking out their meager lives in obscure corners of society,
the conscience of their society. By speaking out their own minds hon-
estly, they succeeded in grasping the very nature of the civilization in
which they lived in ways which were possible to none other of their
contemporaries. Of course, it was only in the case of a few writers that
these feelings and impressions reached the stature of true criticism of
civilization, and most of the writers did not even analyze clearly the
nature of the sufferings which they felt.

The novel of the Meiji and Taisho periods may have developed only
weakly and insufficiently as an expression of the *Zeitgeist*. As an art form,
it probably became trapped in the *cul-de-sac* which it entered. Nevertheless, it was certainly a conscientious, honest voice, a voice depicting
the living countenance of its contemporary human beings discarding all
ostentation and pretense. This is the minimal condition for the modern
novel to be valid fiction, and the Japanese novelists succeeded in fulfilling
this condition in their own way.

CHAPTER I

Gesaku Writing of the Early Meiji Period

As everyone knows, the new Meiji Japan took as its theme the assimilation of Western civilization. In fact, it owed its very being to the transplantation of Western civilization. However, in the "civilization" imported from the West, literature was definitely not included, at least during the initial periods.

When Tsubouchi Shôyô published his *Tôsei Shosei Katagi* (Character of Modern Students), Fukuzawa Yukichi, the representative thinker of the early Meiji period, is reported to have remarked indignantly: "It is quite beneath the dignity of a person holding a Bachelor of Arts degree to engage in such a vulgar occupation as the writing of novels."

Although the authenticity of this episode is somewhat dubious, at least the fact that such a story could gain currency without seeming at all unnatural has a certain symbolic significance. This episode points up quite vividly a number of aspects of the contemporary situation: first, the nature of the "civilization" advocated by Fukuzawa and his like; secondly, the significance of the revolt of the young Tsubouchi, who dared to rebel against the common-sense attitudes of his period; and thirdly, the actual quality of Tsubouchi's work, which created a sensation, not because of its contents, but rather because it was written by an author holding the title of Bachelor of Arts.

Both Fukuzawa and Tsubouchi made outstanding contributions to the Meiji enlightenment and to the introduction of Western culture. However, there was an age difference of twenty years between them, and they both lived according to different systems of values. In the inaugural issue of the periodical *Shigarami sôshi,* Mori Ôgai wrote:

"As Western learning began to penetrate eastward, first only the thing was transmitted to the neglect of the spirit. Learning was limited to the physical sciences, techniques to measurement and the military arts. Everyone realized that the Westerners were a clever race, but no one knew that they were also a virtuous race, let alone that they were a refined race. For this reason, those who devoted themselves to Western learning aimed exclusively at profit and were unhappy unless it led them to enrichment. . . . Nearly all the scholars in the country studied the politics of Plato, rejecting the works of the poets." In this quotation, Mori, who along with Tsubouchi was a great popularizer of the "refined" arts, tells clearly how the tendencies during the early years of the Meiji period appeared to his eyes.

Fukuzawa Yukichi had, it is true, an acute and penetrating understanding of the military prowess of the West and of the intellectual powers on which it was based. He also understood clearly the "dynamic character of the populace" which had built up Western society. Nevertheless, although he visited Occidental countries on several occasions, he never exhibited even the slightest interest in or sympathy for their arts.

On a visit abroad as an official of the shogunate, he remarked that he was convulsed with uncontrollable laughter upon witnessing the dancing. Throughout his life, he never revised this opinion, and in writing of his admiration for things Western, he pointed out clearly that he was definitely not intoxicated at the sight of the beauties of Western art.

This attitude toward literature was, rather than a quirk in the character of Fukuzawa as an individual, a feature characteristic of the life of the early Meiji period itself. This was, after all, a period when Japan had been forced to revise its policy of national isolation under the menace of foreign naval attack. Under the insistent pressure of the "world powers," the people of the period regarded it as their urgent mission to adopt Western civilization as a means of saving their country from doom. It was only natural that people living under such circumstances should regard the quintessence of modern civilization as consisting solely in such things as the invention of the steam engine and the telegraph, the postal system

and modern printing techniques, improved medical techniques, manu-
facturing industries, and the adoption of new political and economic
theories. The transplantation of Western civilization, which was carried
out during the early Meiji period from the sole standpoint of usefulness
to the state, was actually a revolution of an intensity and rapidity surpassing the imagination of persons living in subsequent periods. In this
connection, the extreme utilitarianism of the ideas of the intellectual
leaders who dominated the Meiji enlightenment had something of the
thoroughgoing, intolerant nature of ideologies prevalent in all revolutionary periods. They simply had no time for such "useless" things as
novels.

Viewed from an overall vantage point, this was the tragicomedy of
a people undergoing an enforced self-transformation under the mighty
onslaughts of an incoming alien civilization. The process was later characterized as an "externally induced enlightenment," which, as Natsume
Sôseki remarked, "had to be carried out, as if by someone who has suddenly been deprived of his autonomous faculties and is violently pushed
ahead by someone else. Only by performing unquestioningly the forcible
dictates of the other is he able to move forward." In a certain sense, one
can see even today traces of this "externally induced enlightenment" in
the attitude of viewing only the utilitarian aspects of Western civilization
as "necessary." One example of this was the bureaucratic controls over
book imports during the Second World War. It was permitted to import
Western books on science and technology, but books of literature were
completely forbidden.

Thus, this idea in the minds of the leaders of the Meiji enlightenment
that literature was "unnecessary" remained alive until later periods as a
sort of English-type utilitarianism cum Confucianism. It formed the
basis of the thinking of the politicians of the Meiji period, and all of Meiji
fiction after Tsubouchi, including both the Kenyûsha movement and
naturalism, consistently developed as various forms of revolt against this
socially predominant common-sense attitude.

During the early years of Meiji, when this aspect of the period's character appeared in its most pronounced form, Western "civilization," far from producing a new literature, on the contrary merely exerted a withering influence on the existing literature. Fiction, known then as *gesaku* or flippant writings, had not been treated as serious literature during the Edo period, and was barely able to maintain itself in existence secluded in obscure corners of society during the early Meiji period.

In 1872, Kanagaki Robun and Jôno Arito, on behalf of the *gesakusha* of the time, submitted a petition to the Department of Education complaining that the writing of novels, which had provided a means of livelihood since the days of Santô Kyôden (1761–1816), had suddenly declined of late. "At the present time," they said, "the number has dwindled down to the two of us as well as two or three others." The reason for this state of affairs, they opined, was the advance of knowledge. "As knowledge has been increasing with each passing day and month, people have come to despise vulgar novels as falsehoods and delusions."

In this statement, they themselves admit that their profession of *gesaku* writing had reached a state verging on utter extinction because of the progress being made by society and the advanced knowledge which people were assimilating. Besides revealing the whimsical, unconventional nature of these writers themselves, this admission also provides us with a clear insight into the nature of the "civilization" of their times and into the position to which the writers had been relegated by it in the rapidly changing society.

Even more interesting, however, is that this self-abasement of the writers may, from one point of view, furnish a hint about the tactics which they proposed to adopt in order to assimilate themselves to the changing times. Having sensed that the people of the time had come to "despise vulgar novels as falsehoods and delusions," they began to seek a way out in recording the actualities of the contemporary society. It is a common feature of all periods of revolutionary change that facts, especially the latest facts, appeal most strongly to the liking of the populace.

In his *Meiji Bungaku Shi* (History of Meiji Literature), Honma Hisao writes:

"During the initial period of the Meiji Enlightenment . . . there were practically no works possessing the form of novels. Most of the works dating to that period were merely conglomerations of current satire. In other words, the first decade of the Meiji period, ending in 1877, was a period which forced even writers like Robun or Ôga, who had already been established novelists before the Meiji period, to give up writing their novels and to write such satirical ephemera . . . The period was one lacking the mental composure to enjoy the reading of novels."

The only thing which the novelists could do, from their accustomed "despised" corner in society which they had occupied since the period of the old shogunate, was to depict, in a manner calculated to appeal to the casual interest, the externals of the new era from the viewpoint of a bystander, and to color their observations with a light satirical touch. This tendency did not apply merely to the *gesakusha*. As will be mentioned later, it applied also to ephemeral prose in Chinese *(gebun)* and to humorous poems in Chinese and Japanese *(kyôshi, kyôka)*. Writers in all of these different genres delighted in applying irony and humor against the background of social conditions during the Meiji "enlightenment." Such *gesakusha* as Kanagaki Robun, Mantei Ôga, and Takabatake Ransen all played active roles during this period and succeeded in living through this period of tribulations until the *gesaku* was later revived when the "little" newspapers began to be published. Robun's novel *Aguranabe*, published in 1871, is the representative work in this style.

Aguranabe is a work written in the same vein as *Ukiyo-buro*. Persons from various social classes are depicted, chiefly through their conversations, as they come together at a restaurant serving beef dishes, a great novelty at the time. As the custom of eating beef served as a symbol of "enlightenment" for the people of the early Meiji period, it was a topic of interest to all, and the various characters who appear in the restaurant —a person of "Western" tastes, a country samurai, an artisan, a *soi-disant* scholar, a geisha, an actor, a quack doctor, etc.—represent the styles of colloquial speech of persons of all levels of society. Thus, the dialogue in itself presents an extremely animated picture of the manners and customs of the times. Besides, the typical features of various types of characters are carefully distinguished, although in a stereotyped fashion. For these reasons, the work can stand to be read again today, not merely as a source document for the history of manners and customs. The wit and skill of the author are evident throughout the work, and it is no wonder that it has so often been recommended as the typical *gesaku* novel of this period.

Nevertheless, all of the works of these *gesakusha* lack a fundamental understanding of the new era, and the satire and negation contained in them are shallow and superficial. Their vulgar humor is intended merely as entertainment and has neither a destructive nor a constructive message. In this sense, they have made no progress at all beyond the levels reached by the *gesaku* novels of the past.

Robun himself, in his petition to the Department of Education which was quoted above, writes that *gesaku* novels are "not written to be shown to the learned, but are rather for the edification of the unlearned." He also refers to himself as a "base person of a lowly occupation." This alone would be sufficient to convince us that their works would be quite unworthy reading for members of the intelligentsia, for whom they would be, if anything, merely means of killing time.

The "learned" persons of the period, who were members of the samurai class or their young protégés, read for enjoyment, rather than these works of the *gesakusha,* ephemeral works called *gebun,* satirical works about the customs and mores of the times written by scholars and literary men in Chinese prose. Two representative works of this type were *Tôkyô Shin Hanjô Ki* (Record of the New Prosperity of Tokyo) (1874) by Hattori Bushô and *Ryûkyô shinshi Dainihen* (New Description of Yanagibashi, Second Installment) (1874) by Narushima Ryûhoku. *Tôkyô Shin Hanjô Ki* was a book describing the social conditions during the "enlightenment" period in terms of various places in Tokyo. In style it was patterned after a book called *Edo Hanjô Ki* (Record of the Prosperity of Edo) by Terakado Seiken, which was published during the 1830's. *Ryûkyô Shinshi Dainihen* also was written in the same style as these "records of prosperity." The first installment had already been published in 1859.

The second installment satirized the current situation in the guise of describing the changes undergone by the geisha in the gay quarters of Yanagibashi.

Although the style of these books was not particularly novel, they evoked a humorous feeling by treating commonplace incidents in the prosaic world in Chinese prose, a style quite out of harmony with the subject matter in question. Since most of these writers were former retainers of the old shogunate or former samurai now in straightened circumstances, their satire and irony were much sharper and more spirited than those of the *gesakusha*—although even they cannot escape the charge of superficiality. For this reason, they were read with great enthusiasm by the contemporary reading public.

In his novel *Gan* (The Wild Goose), Mori Ôgai wrote that the hero Okada, a medical student, "greatly enjoyed reading books written in verse by Chinese scholars about the latest happenings in the new society."

Subsequently, both Hattori and Narushima became the editors of magazines and newspapers, retaining their literary fame for many years. Narushima was the president of a newspaper called the Chôya Shimbun, to which he contributed critical articles. In 1877 he also founded a literary review called the *Kagetsu Shinshi,* in which he published many articles which further enhanced his literary stature. In talent and learning, Hattori was no equal of Narushima. Nevertheless, the *Tôkyô Shinshi,* a review which he edited, enjoyed an equal popularity to the *Kagetsu Shinshi* until the former was suppressed by the government in 1883.

Japanese modern fiction is said to be lacking in the elements of humor and satire. However, although this judgment is valid for the period after 1887, especially after the rise of naturalism, it does not apply at all to the period before that, particularly to the years before 1877, as we have just seen.

On the contrary, all of the prose works of this period—both the *gebun* works intended for the "learned" reader and the *gesaku* works intended for the "unlearned"—are devoted exclusively to satire and humor. What were the reasons for this, and why were these elements lost later? These are questions deserving serious consideration.

No doubt the following may be considered among the possible ex-
planations. First of all, the writers of all the contemporary *gesaku* and
gebun literature were persons in the position of bystanders nursing feelings
of near-hostility toward the new times. Besides, they were keenly aware
of their own powerlessness. Their readers were also aware—to varying
degrees, of course—that they, too, were playing parts as actors in this
unprecedented political and cultural comedy. Like all periods of political
upheaval, the early Meiji years were a time when betrayal, the pursuit
of personal advantage, and opportunism ran rampant. The adherents of
the Imperial party, who had until then advocated "expulsion of the bar-
barians," once they came to power immediately switched to a policy of
opening the country. Former adherents of the old shogunate became
officials in the new government. The government officials, self-com-
placently regarding themselves as the representatives of "civilization,"
led lives of luxury and disorder. All of this could not but arouse the
antipathy and sense of humor of the populace. In addition to this, the
numerous products of Western civilization which had been transplanted
to Japan by high-handed governmental authority were imported much
too quickly for them to be assimilated at leisure. Inevitably, these items
were grafted onto Japanese life in awkward forms completely out of
harmony with the previous living patterns of the people. On one hand,
the people were kept constantly dazzled by the magic of this newly imported "civilization," while on the other hand they had to endure the
chaos engendered in their lives by this hastily introduced alien culture.
They endured it by regarding both themselves and others around them
as characters in a comedy. Thus, the "enlightenment" period of the first
years of the Meiji era was a period when the essential nature of subsequent
Meiji civilization was displayed in its most unvarnished form. The features which appeared at this time subsequently became, in modified
forms, the distinctive features of Meiji civilization. In a sense, the year
still present today.

Consequently, as for the reason why humor and satire disappeared
from literature, one explanation is that literature itself underwent Western influence, becoming another aspect of the "enlightenment" phenom-

enon. Literature ceased to be merely a spectator of the comedy; it itself had become one of the characters.

However, there were some men of letters who, with their deeper understanding of Western civilization, became aware of the comical nature of this period. It is a noteworthy fact that writers like Natsume Sôseki and Nagai Kafû, both masters of "criticism of civilization," were at the same time either practitioners or advocates of humorous literature.

Interestingly, during the Shôwa period, Masamune Hakuchô wrote as follows.

"I think that our contemporary manners and customs, literature, and ideas have always been, ever since the Meiji period, nothing but a steady process of constant hasty imitation of the West. This is just as true today as it was then. Each succeeding period has always been nothing but a series of new "Enlightenments." "

When we facilely dismiss the past with contempt, we think that we have thus escaped from it. Masamune sensed that, the more we neglect the past, the more persistently will it come back, ghost-like, to haunt us with its continual presence.

CHAPTER II

The Political Novel and the Translated Novel

The decade from about 1877 to about 1887 may be called the season of the political novel. In the wake of the Seinan Rebellion, the last armed revolt on the part of the disgruntled samurai class, society as a whole entered a period of relatively stable construction. During this period, opposition politicians, realizing the impossibility of overthrowing the government by armed force, attempted to attain their aims and correct the misdeeds of the ruling bureaucracy by the power of the spoken and printed word. Newspapers and reviews grew extremely rapidly, and their influence came to govern the public opinion of the entire nation. The government, on its part, soon established a newspaper law and a libel law in order to control the press. Prominent newspaper writers such as Narushima Ryûhoku, Suehiro Tetchô, and Fujita Mokichi were often jailed under these laws.

The newspapers at this period were divided into the so-called "big" newspapers and "little" newspapers. This distinction was not necessarily one of the business scope of the newspapers, but rather reflected the contents. The big newspapers were read by the intelligentsia; their editorials dealt chiefly with politics; and their news items also laid chief emphasis on politics and economics. On the other hand, the little newspapers carried no editorials, paid little attention to political opinion or political news items, and aimed at a broader range of readers by concentrating chiefly on commonplace incidents in the everyday world and on news of the demimonde and the world of entertainment.

Some of these "little" newspapers, such as the *Yomiuri Shimbun*, the

Hiragana E-iri Shimbun, and the *Kanayomi Shimbun,* had space for serial novels. It was here that Kanagaki Robun, Takabatake Ransen, and numerous *gesakusha* in narrow circumstances were able to find a means of livelihood. The works published in these newspapers developed from mere "conglomerations of ephemeral satire" into writings in a documentary vein in fictional form. The "documentary" writings which were written in such profusion at that time sometimes drew on historical materials, while others dealt with current events and ordinary news stories. The historical stories were set chiefly during the Meiji Restoration, while the latter stories dealt with a variety of contemporary scandals. For instance, there was a whole series of works recounting the careers of wicked women and murderesses such as Takahashi O-den, Yoarashi O-kinu, and Torioi O-matsu. Others were stories about vendettas, which were still being practiced at that time. Still others were fictionalized versions of love suicides or murders which had just happened. Incidents in the Seinan Rebellion were also dealt with in a thoroughly sensational manner.

The most prominent writers of these stories were Kanagaki Robun and Takabatake Ransen, as well as the Kanagaki School and the Ryûtei School, which centered around the personalities of these two writers. (The Ryûtei School, which centered around Takabatake Ransen, derived its name from the fact that Takabatake assumed the pen name of Ryûtei Tanehiko II.) There was also the Tamenaga School of Somesaki Nobufusa and other writers maintaining the tradition of *ninjô-bon* fiction. Even Tsubouchi Shôyô, who was responsible for the final flowering of *gesaku* literature and later ushered in the new era of Meiji literature, writes in his memoirs that, when he first came to Tokyo around 1877, he was drawn to Kanagaki Robun by the latter's fame and even thought of asking for an introduction to Kanagaki with the intention of becoming a protégé.

Nevertheless, from today's vantage point, the central trend in the fiction of the period was not these writings for the purpose of entertainment, but rather the political novel and the translated novel, which reflected so well the mental consciousness of the period. These novels possess contents which are much closer to those of contemporary fiction than one would imagine; and they also make up the basis on which Tsubouchi Shôyô and Futabatei Shimei effected their literary reforms.

In the preceding chapter, I wrote that the national leaders immediately after the Meiji Restoration were indifferent to Western letters and fine arts. However, as the conditions in Western countries gradually became better known, and especially as the number of students who had studied abroad and persons who had been overseas on tours of inspection increased, there was an inevitable growing awareness that the letters, the fine arts, and the drama occupied in the Western countries a position entirely different from that in Japan, and that remarkable importance was attached to them in both public and private life. This led them to reflect on the position to which the arts as a whole were relegated in Japan and on the contents of the arts, and the movement for "improving" the arts ensued as an inevitable consequence.

At the same time, the leaders of the "enlightenment" could not afford to ignore the strong impact on readers of the concrete images created by stories and the printed word in the broad sense. Even Fukuzawa Yukichi in 1872 published what he called "a sort of novel" called *Katawa Musume* (The Maimed Maiden), in which he urged the abolition of the custom of blackening the teeth of women. In the same year, Fukuzawa also translated a collection of homilies from England under the title of *Dômô Oshiegusa* (Instructive Leaves for the Edification of Children). These also may be called an anthology of homiletic short stories.

Samuel Smiles' *Self-help*, translated by Nakamura Masanao, was published in 1871 under the title *Saikoku Risshi Hen* (Sketches of Self-made Men of the West). As the title of the translation suggests, it is a collection of biographical sketches taken from historical characters, contemporary inventors and reformers, and various segments of society. The examples are all chosen to illustrate the necessity of independent study and indomitable will power. This book, which was comparable with *Gakumon no susume* (The Encouragement of Learning) by Fukuzawa Yukichi in the extent and profundity of its influence, affected the contemporary young men who read it almost as intensely as a novel would. The impact of the book can be judged by the fact that two episodes taken from it were dramatized and performed on the stage two years after its publication.

Thus, when the living patterns of Occidentals were brought to the attention of the Japanese as near-to-home patterns for them to emulate, it was only natural that the young men studying the "Western learning" in preparation for brilliant careers in the new age should wish to understand, not only the political and economic activities of Westerners, but also their emotional life. The first full-scale answer to their curiosity was a book by Niwa Jun'ichirô entitled *Ôshû kiji Karyû Shunwa* (1878) (Strange Story from Europe: A Spring Tale of Flowers and Willows), which purported to be a translation of the general plot of the English novel *Ernest Maltravers* by Bulwer-Lytton and its sequel. The novel is a stereotyped love story involving a talented boy from a good family who loves an ill-fated beauty. At the beginning, strange coincidence brings the hero and heroine together; they fall in love, and are finally reunited after many vicissitudes. The conventional plot was easy to accept for readers familiar with the old-fashioned Japanese stories. Besides, the depiction of the love customs of the Westerners appealed strongly to the curiosity of contemporary Japanese readers. For this reason, Bulwer-Lytton's other novels were also translated in the time to come, and other novels by many other Western writers also found their way into print in Japanese translations with flowery and vaguely erotic titles such as "Tale of Passion in the Spring Wind," "Strange Tales of the Spring Window," or "Spring Tale of the Pair of Love-birds."

The translator Niwa Jun'ichirô had gone to study in England in 1868 as the companion of Sanjô Kimitomi, the son of the aristocratic statesman Sanjô Sanetomi. However, because of his dissolute conduct and his bad influence on the son, he fell under the displeasure of the boy's father, who blocked his way into a governmental career. His hopes of political advancement destroyed, Niwa decided on a literary career and spent the rest of his life as a journalist. As the motive for translating Bulwer-Lytton's novel, Tanba claimed that he wished to provide students of English history with interesting information about "English manners and customs in recent ages." However, his real motive was probably rebellion against the oppressive atmosphere of utilitarianism prevalent at that time. The facts that he requested Hattori Bushô to revise the manuscript of the translation and that the work was published with a preface by Narushima Ryûhoku reveal clearly that *Karyû Shunwa* is in the tradition of the *gebun* described in the previous chapter.

In the same sense, the following statements by Ryûhoku in his preface to the book are also worthy of attention.

"The entire world and all things in it are a world of passion. The learned bigots say that in Western countries the people are concerned with profit, speak only of useful things, and do not care about the refinements and affairs of passion. This is a most pernicious distortion. I have traveled abroad for one year and have myself seen that their passions and ours correspond perfectly, that there is not the slightest difference between us and them. . . . Those learned bigots, besides, unfailingly question the usefulness of tales of passion, which they dismiss merely as leading to moral depravity and a wicked life. In my opinion, we are men of passion born into this world of passion; and therefore we read tales of passion. This is, indeed, the gift of our Creator. Are not men the same as the grass and the trees? . . . What do you think, you young men of talent in the world?"

In this preface, deriding the "pernicious distortion" of the utilitarianism of the "learned bigots," Ryûhoku argues that "the entire world and all things in it are a world of passion," that it is the "gift of our Creator" that we "read tales of passion." In these ideas, we see foreshadowed the ideas of *Shôsetsu Shinzui* of Tsubouchi Shôyô, which advocated the liberation of literature from the utilitarian viewpoint.

Of course, this attitude does not go beyond a sarcastic criticism of the times and probably does not deserve to be regarded as serious literary theory. However, in Ryûhoku's view, the Westerners are human. Being human, they love. Thus, it is quite clear that his view is much more accurate and natural than the ideas of the "learned bigots," who see in the West nothing but a model of profitableness and usefulness to be emulated. As soon as this current of thought matures sufficiently and begins to assert itself clearly, it will certainly lead to a new literary movement based on something other than utilitarianism.

In this sense, it is interesting that Tsubouchi Shôyô was the translator of *Shunpû Jôwa* (Tale of Passion in the Spring Wind), a translation of Sir Walter Scott's *Bride of Lammermoor,* published in 1880 under the pseudonym of Tachibana Kenzô. Besides, Tsubouchi worked together with Takata Sanae and Amano Tameyuki on a joint translation of *Shunsô Kiwa* (Strange Tales of the Spring Window), which was published in 1884. The latter was a translation of Scott's *Lady of the Lake* and was edited by Hattori Bushô.

Other Western works which were translated for Japanese readers in the form of *ninjô-bon* novels were: *Ôshû Jôfu Gunpô Kiwa* (European Tales of Passion: Strange Stories of Assorted Beauties) (1882, translated by Ôkubo Kanzaburô), a selection from the *Decameron; Sôfuren* (Conjugal Longing) (1886, translated by Sano Takashi), also an elaboration of an episode from the *Decameron;* and *Rokoku Kibun Kashin Chôshi Roku* (Strange Story from Russia: Record of Flowery Hearts and Butterfly Thoughts) (1883), a translation of Pushkin's *Captain's Daughter* by Takasu Jisuke. Also, *Kaikan Kyôki Arabiya Monogatari* (Amazing from the Start: Arabian Tales), a selection from the Arabian Nights translated by Nagamine Hideki in 1875, falls into this general category. Besides these, there were translations of adventure stories by Jules Verne, such as *Shinsetsu Hachijûnichikan Sekai Isshû* (New Story: Around the World in Eighty Days) (1878, translated by Kawashima Chûnosuke); *Kyûjûshichi Jikan Nijippun Tsuki Sekai Ryokô* (Voyage to the Moon in 97 Hours and 20 Minutes) (1880, translated by Inoue Tsutomu); and *Rokuman Kairi Kaitei Kikô* (Sixty Thousand Leagues Under the Sea) (1884, translated by Inoue Tsutomu). These adventure stories were read out of popular wonderment at the feats of science and technology or merely out of curiosity in things Western in general.

However, the greatest number of contemporary translated fiction was novels dealing with Western politicians or political incidents. At that time, public opinion was extremely agitated over the convening of the Imperial Diet, and the popular rights movement had reached its zenith.

It was probably for this reason that current interest in the West tended to center around political themes. A very large proportion of these works dealt with the French Revolution or with the Russian Nihilists; this fact reflected the radical tendencies which had become general among the intelligentsia of the period.

Fénelon's *Télémaque* was partially translated by Miyajima Shunshô in 1879 and published under the title *Ôshû Shôsetsu Teremaku Kafuku Dan* (European Novel: The Vicissitudes of Telemague). This translation is famous as being an unusually early introduction of a French classic. It was chosen evidently because the part containing instructions for the ruler appealed to the current tastes of the Japanese reading public.

Another noteworthy translation was that of Sir Thomas More's *Utopia*, published in 1882 under the title *Ryôseifu Dan* (Story of Good Government). In the same year were published a summarized translation of the court hearings in the case of Vera Zaslich, *Rokoku Kibun Retsujo no Gigoku* (Strange Story from Russia: Tribulations of a Heroic Woman) (translated by Somada Sakutarô); *Kyomutô Taiji Kidan* (Strange Tale of the Subjugation of the Nihilists), a translation by Kawashima Chûnosuke of a book originally written by Paul Vernier; free translations of two novels by Dumas, *Furansu Kakumei Ki Jiyû no Gaika* (Story of the French Revolution: Triumphal Song of Freedom) (translated by Miyazaki Muryû) and *Kakumei Kigen Seiyô Chishio no Sayoarashi* (Origins of the Revolution: Bloody Night Storm in the West) (translated by Sakurada Hyakuei); and a translation of the first half of Schiller's *Wilhelm Tell* published under the title *Teru Jiyû Dan* (Tell: Story of Freedom). It is evident that the year 1882, during which the democratic political leader Itagaki Taisuke was wounded by a would-be assassin and the Fukushima incident occured, was also the high-water mark in the publication of books of this type.

Some of the works of Shakespeare were treated in the *ninjô-bon* fashion. For instance, there were two translations of *Romeo and Juliet*. One was called *Shunjô Ukiyo no Yume* (Spring Passion: Dream of the Floating World) (1886, translated by Kawashima Keizô), and the other *Seiyô Musume Setsuyô* (Western Girl's Handbook) (1887, translated by Kinoshita Shinzaburô). On the other hand, other works were treated in the manner of political novels. *Julius Caesar* was translated by Tsubouchi Shôyô in 1883 under the title of *Jiyû no Tachi Nagori no Kireaji* (Remaining Sharpness of the Sword of Freedom), and *The Merchant of Venice* was translated as *Jinniku Shichi-ire Saiban* (Human Flesh Pawning Trial). Evidently general interest was aroused by the work because it dealt with a Western trial. This also reflects the general intellectual atmosphere of the times.

The young intellectuals of this period were widely seized by a passionate interest in politics. The political novel, which rose and declined almost in unison with the People's Rights movement during the period of approximately two decades beginning around 1877, dealt with different types of subject matter, and in form there were great qualitative and quantitative variations. In general, however, these were novels in which the hero was a person representing the political ideals of the author, and all the other characters appearing in the novel were also embodiments of various concepts. In this respect, the Meiji political novel differs radically in its nature from the novels written after Tsubouchi Shôyô, which were rooted in the naturalistic depiction of reality.

For this reason, the political novels are often dismissed today as being works antedating real literature or amateurish works written by politicians for their own pleasure. However, they were more than this.

The People's Rights movement of that period contained within itself numerous feudalistic elements, and in the final analysis it moved towards collapse and compromise on account of its own internal weaknesses. Like the People's Rights movement, the political novels of the time also contained fundamental defects which prevented them from becoming the immediate matrix of a truly modern fiction. Nevertheless, these novels deserve to be re-evaluated as a special form of Romantic literature, for they were able to capture the hearts and minds of the young men of the time engaged in the building of a new Japan with a profundity and a breadth to which no literary movement in later period can lay claim.

In the *Kindai Nihon Bungaku Kôza* (Anthology of Lectures on Modern Japanese Literature), Odagiri Hideo writes that the People's Rights movement of this period was something more than a mere political movement. It was a movement aiming at a broader goal: the liberation of modern man. The hearts of the populace, which had been thoroughly aroused by the reforms of the Meiji Restoration, were deeply moved by the appeals of this movement. Everywhere the country was filled with a new vitality, and in every field of life precious new potentialities were perceived. Finally, however, these new potentialities were crushed as the movement collapsed. The political novel, writes Odagiri, directly reflected this character of the People's Rights movement. Odagiri's appraisal reveals clearly the reason why the political novel was able to arouse the romantic enthusiasm of the young men of the time.

For instance, in his *Omoide no Ki* (Recollections), Tokutomi Roka writes: "The times changed like a rising tide. . . . We began to devour voraciously such novels as *Seiyô Chishio no Sayoarashi* and *Jiyû no Gaika*. . . . Then, reading the book *Keikoku Bidan,* there is no telling how many nights we stayed up until dawn, ruining our eyes worrying about the government of the city of Thebes with the heroes Epaminondas and Pelopidas."

As for the reasons why the political novel enjoyed such success—a success which, in a sense, novels of later periods were never to attain— we must first mention the fact, as pointed out by Odagiri, that they gave a most direct expression to the "vitality" of a society, and particularly to its youth, which had been roused from the old ways of the age of feudalism by the unprecedented upheavals of the Meiji Restoration and which was just become aware of new ideas and new ways of life. We today can hardly imagine the effect of the abolition of the feudal class system under the principle of "equality for all four classes"—what a fresh and moving imprint must have been made on the hearts of the contemporary people, and how this event must have aroused their will to live!

The thinkers of the early Meiji enlightenment also, under the influence of this feeling of liberation, dreamed of rapid assimilation of Western things. Thus, for most young men, to master the new civilization was synonymous with a successful career. It was only natural that knowledge and virtue should be propagandized widely as the path to social success.

As mentioned above, the translation of Smiles' *Self-help* was widely read and had a profound influence on the youth. The main idea of this work was that "those who strive diligently in their youth will gain ease and comfort later in life," and the book was written to inspire young men to work and study hard. Fukuzawa's *Gakumon no Susume* (The Encouragement of Learning) was equally popular as a bible of the new age. The latter book contained statements like these: "Men have no inborn distinctions of nobility or baseness and of wealth or poverty. Only those who devote themselves to learning and come to a good understanding of things will be noble and wealthy, while the ignorant will be poor and base."

This type of utilitarianism was especially appealing to the minds of the youngmen of the samurai class, which as a group was largely destined to ruin, since it accorded with the tenets of Confucianism, for which the highest virtue was the exaltation of the family and the provision of security for one's parents.

This worship of wordly success, however, had not yet been corrupted by the vulgar egoism which was attached to it in later periods. At this early period, success merely appeared to everyone to be the first praiseworthy fruit of the new society of social equality. *Self-help* regards the independence of the individual and the independence of the nation as being the products of exactly the same sort of diligence and effort. Fukuzawa also entertained extremely optimistic views in this regard. He wrote: "If all the people earnestly desire learning, understand the principles of things, and move in the paths of civilization . . . then we may certainly expect the nation to be wealthy and strong."

No opposition between the individual and society was at all discernible here. In fact, there was not even any awakening of the individual consciousness in the true sense. Or rather, it might perhaps be more appropriate to say that the awakening of individuality was grasped merely in terms of the possibility of worldly success.

In such a period, it was only to be expected that the enthusiasms of the young should be concentrated in politics. Not only was politics for them the shortcut to a successful career; it was also the arena where they could give vent most directly to their patriotic sentiments. The important thing was that, in their psychological makeup, there was no trace of deception and no sense of contradiction whatsoever.

Let us return to Tokutomi Roka's *Omoide no Ki,* where we find the following reminiscences of this period:

"As I look back on it from today, this period was truly a delightful time. The young men of the day were preparing to make their way straight and unswerving through life, unaware of what the world was really like, unaware of the barriers and pitfalls before them, and unaware of how costly was the price of progress which they themselves and their society as a whole would have to pay. The instructors were young, and the pupils were juvenile. Together they were rushing forward towards their bright, idealistic world."

These words of Tokutomi Roka probably contain no exaggeration. Roka is here describing not only the springtide of his own youth, but also a whole period, the very special springtide of young Japan as it entered the modern age. It was a period when the liberation of the feelings was accomplished merely in terms of political enthusiasms and was confined to a passionate desire for worldly success.

In this sense, the political novel was a very revealing expression of the distorted aspects of this youthful period. In the political novel, the ideas of the enlightenment and the translated novel were all rolled into one. The earliest political novels were mere puerile allegories, such as *Minken Engi Jôkai Haran* (Discourses on People's Rights: Billows on the Seas of Passion) (1880, by Toda Kindô) or *Akoku Mindô Jiyû no Nishiki* (Way of American People: Brocade of Freedom) (1883, by Sakurada Hyakuei). However, within a very short time, the political novel had developed to a remarkable degree, both quantitatively and qualitatively, as a means for expressing the feelings of the intellectuals who were indignant at the trends of the times and who opposed those then in power. Although both had discontent and rebellion as their keynote, the political novel came to have a fundamental character quite different from that of the *gesaku* literature and the *gebun* writings in Chinese. The child of the womb of the new era, the political novel flattered itself that it was one step ahead of reality in expressing the ideas of the era.

Another possible reason why these novels were so widely read by all segments of society was the following. In these political novels, there was no characterization of the personages as real human beings in the modern sense. All the characters appearing in these novels were basically nothing but stereotypes which did not conflict with the feudalistic thinking which still dominated the society of the period.

Among the early political novels, the most enthusiastically received by the public was *Kajin no Kigû* (Strange Encounters with Beautiful Women) (1885), published by Shiba Shirô under the pseudonym of Tôkai Sanshi. However, even in this novel, the personages make an extremely weak impression in comparison with the vast scope of the work itself. The romance between the hero and the two women Mystic Orchid and Crimson Lotus, which begins with their first encounter on the "Tower of Independence in Philadelphia," has not the slightest touches of realism. From start to finish, the hero remains a gentleman of the "patriot consumed with righteous indignation" type, and the center of interest in the story soon shifts to a series of extraneous characters, whom the author introduces quite willfully. These characters tell the history of the downfall of various small countries in modern world history. Rather than the progress of a romantic love story, the contemporary readers were evidently much more fascinated by the story of how countries like Hungary and Madagascar lost their independence.

Equally popular among youthful readers was a book called *Keikoku Bidan* (Laudable Anecdotes of Able Statesmanship) (1883) by Yano Ryû-kei. In his preface, the author tells his readers that the book was assembled by translating selections from various books describing famous incidents in ancient Greek history. "The happenings are not distorted fancifully as is done in ordinary novels, and there is no attempt to confuse right and wrong or good and evil. The actual happenings are presented with only a slight amount of embellishment." As readers pored absorbedly over these accounts of heroes who exerted themselves for the glory of Thebes, their fascination was no doubt enhanced by the notion that these accounts were not imaginary. In the deeds of these Greek generals, taken largely from English history textbooks, the readers must have sensed a well-proportioned mixture of Oriental heroics with democratic ideas. Epaminondas was no doubt a character personifying the ideals of contemporary readers more exactly than any other hero in the fiction currently being read in Japan.

Rather than fiction, these works more closely resembled ancient or contemporary history, and the characters depicted in them were extremely ill-defined and stereotyped. These defects reveal that these works antedated the modern novel. At the same time, we can easily comprehend the intensity and the homogeneity of the dreams cherished by both writers and readers.

As Fukuda Eiko recalls in her autobiography *Warawa no Hanshôgai* (My Life), the persons who participated in the People's Rights movement of this period, while belonging to the Jiyûtô (Liberal Party), the most radical of the political parties, nevertheless retained almost completely intact a feudal mentality in their emotional lives. Thus, the political novel may be said to reflect this type of mentality perfectly.

Finally, let it be said that one of the major attractions of the political novels was their style. These novels were written in a style patterned after Chinese prose, called *kanbun* by the Japanese. As a style, it was, of course, not a new one by any means. However, it was the style which best suited the type of education and the spirit of the youths of the period. Thanks to its distinctive rhythms and intonations, this style had the power to intoxicate the reader in a manner which was almost completely lost in the colloquial literary style which became prevalent later. Some may say that this literary style was used to conceal the emptiness of the contents. However, it would be more appropriate to think of this mixed Sino-Japanese style as the last creative outburst of Japan's long tradition of *kanbun* literary expression. One of the fundamental concepts of fiction is that the novel is the creation of fantasy by means of the written word.

This concept of fiction was disregarded, perhaps excessively, by the novelists of naturalism and after. Even though the fantasy created by the political novel lacks human characterization with a truthfulness which would be able to endure the erosion of time, nevertheless the political novel was written in a style which still lives, allowing the reader of today to form a most vivid conception of the spirit of the times.

The better political novels had a sort of epic character. From this standpoint, the most typical of the political novels would be those like *Keikoku Bidan* and *Kajin no Kigû,* which scarcely bothered to meet the stylistic requirements of the novel. However, when we come to the later political novels, which are outfitted with all the externals of the novel, such as *Setchûbai* (Plum Tree in the Snow, 1886) and *Kakan no Uguisu* (Nightingale amid the Flowers, 1887) by Suehiro Tetchô, and *Ryokusadan* (Tale of the Green Raincoat, 1886) and *Shinsô no Kajin* (Beauty in Modern Garb, 1887) by Sudô Nansui, we notice rather the stereotyped characters and the watered-down style. When we re-read these later novels today, they appear to be too much like fiction, and there is little of interest to us in them.

In sum, the political novel was a reflection of the abortive People's Rights movement. As such, it had its many defects. However, as Kataoka Ryôichi has pointed out, "literature, which had until then been exclusively the property of the *gesakusha,* passed into the hands of the intellectuals, who used it to deal earnestly with the important problems of human life. In this sense, the rise of the political novel was of great significance. It meant clearly a revolution in literature." The political novel ought to be accorded a value and a significance much greater than it is commonly given today.

Even after the literary revolution accomplished by Tsubouchi Shôyô and the resulting formation of the so-called *bundan* centering around the Kenyûsha, novels of this type continued regardless to be loved for a long time by young readers. The final installment of *Kajin no Kigû* appeared in 1897, and the novels of Yano Ryûkei and Suehiro Tetchô also continued to have their devoted youthful readers for a long time.

CHAPTER III

*Shôsetsu Shinzui and Tôsei Shosei Katagi
and Tsubouchi Shôyô*

In 1885, Tsubouchi Shôyô, a 26-year old bachelor of literature *(bungakushi)* who had graduated from Tokyo University two years before, published his *Ichidoku Santan Tôsei Shosei Katagi* (Read and Deplore: Character of Modern Students) under the fanciful pseudonym of "Bungakushi Harunoya Oboro." Later in the same year, he also published his pamphlet entitled *Shôsetsu shinzui* (The Essence of the Novel). One hardly need discuss here once again the great significance which these two works have in the history of modern Japanese letters. In the past, it was taken for granted that the history of Meiji fiction began at this very point. Indeed, one can scarcely overemphasize the revolutionary significance of the achievements of the young Tsubouchi, who was the first to transplant to Japan the concept of the modern novel in a well-delineated form and who also himself provided an actual example of how this concept could be applied.

However, because of the very profound influence of the work of Tsubouchi on the formation and on the nature of subsequent Japanese fiction, it behooves us to establish clearly both the meaning and the limitations of the reforms which he carried out. This is a task of the utmost importance, transcending mere historical reminiscence.

It is said that in everything the beginning is the most important period. The formative period in Japanese fiction in the years before and after 1887—the years which gave birth to Tsubouchi Shôyô, Futabatei Shimei, Ozaki Kôyô, Kôda Rohan, Mori Ôgai, and Yamada Bimyô—had the same importance for modern Japanese fiction as the youthful period of the twenties have in the lifetime of a human being.

Throughout his life, Tsubouchi was a persistent popularizer of knowledge and an educator. As such, he left a profound imprint on the history of his nation. Besides his work in the field of fiction, he made many other pioneering contributions in the reform of the drama and in the translation and introduction of English literature. However, as a person he was a moderate, temperate man of good sense lacking both the lopsidedness and the inner tragedy which one so often finds in reformers.

Why, then, was it precisely he who accomplished the most significant revolution in the whole history of Meiji literature? It was because of the position in which he had placed himself—the ambiguous, contradictory position of a Tokyo University student well-versed in the *gesaku* literature. Both the rapid success of Tsubouchi's literary reforms and the limitations of his accomplishments are explained by the fact that these reforms were achieved chiefly as a result of the energines generated by this position which he occupied.

Tsubouchi was born into a family of samurai belonging to the Owari clan. Until his middle school days, he grew up in Nagoya, and even before going to Tokyo he was thoroughly familiar with the *gesaku* literature of the later Edo period and with the Kabuki drama.

In his *Kaioku Mandan* (Random Recollections) he says: "Although I was brought up in the country, I was familiar since my youth with the *gesaku* literature of the Bunka and Bunsei periods (1804–1829). Therefore, as soon as I came to Tokyo, I was immediately able to appreciate the arts of Edo and the distinctive fascination of Edo and its ways no less than a person who had been born in the city." Ichijima Shunjô, one of Tsubouchi's university friends, recalled that Tsubouchi once showed him a list of more than a thousand book titles, including *yomi-bon, share-bon, ninjô-bon,* and even the illustrated story books called *kusa-zôshi*. Tsubouchi explained that this was a list of most of the books which he had read while living in Nagoya. Ichijima remembers being astonished at the profundity of Tsubouchi's familiarity with Edo literature.

During his university days, Tsubouchi was admittedly a young man with a nature approaching frivolity. Recalling this period in his life at a later date, he wrote that he was then a *"gokuraku-tonbo"* (a dragonfly of paradise, i.e., a carefree, flippant person) and that he "seemed like a person who was constantly inebriated." Together with students sharing the same tastes, he formed a coterie of young men who were constantly going on outings, visiting theaters and frequenting vaudeville houses and restaurants. These students were reportedly frowned upon by the serious students at Tokyo University, which had by then come very much to resemble a training school for future government officials.

However, this coterie also included some who used to read foreign novels. Stimulated by upperclassmen like Okakura Kakuzô (Tenshin) and Fukutomi Kôki and by his classmates Tan Otsuma and Takada Sanae, Tsubouchi began to read novels by Dumas, Lytton, Scott, Hugo, and Poe. He came to be a sort of expert on Western novels, and even during school lectures he would continue to study Chaucer, Shakespeare, Milton, and Spencer. Going to the library, he would zealously read criticisms of English literature. Gradually he came to realize, albeit only vaguely, how the Western concepts of literature and attitudes toward society differed from those prevalent in Japan, and he soon formed the idea of elevating Japanese fiction to the level of a branch of art, understood in this sense.

Both *Shôsetsu Shinzui* and *Tôsei Shosei Katagi* may be regarded as manifestations of this desire. Particularly the following words in the Preface to *Shôsetsu Shinzui* may be considered a clear formulation of such intentions: "I desire henceforth to work for the improvement and advancement of Japanese fiction with the aim of seeing it eventually surpassing European novels and occupying a brilliant position among the arts, together with painting, music, and poetry." It was also for this reason that Tsubouchi began this epoch-making work with arguments aiming to "prove clearly that the novel is art."

The argument of *Shôsetsu Shinzui* may be summarized more or less as follows: "The novel is an art form. It is an art form in the sense in which 'art' is understood in the West." This simple assertion was indeed a most radical innovation in comparison with the ideas commonly accepted in those days, as we shall see below.

The novelty of this idea consisted in its insistence that the novel was an art form and that art ought to be highly esteemed in civilized society. This assertion went straight against the Confucian prejudices inherited from the Edo period, when novels were despised as the province of the *gesakusha,* the writers of "flippant letters."

It is almost impossible for us to imagine the significance of this idea today, when writers and actors have come to be respected almost as much as they are in Western society. Until the Meiji Restoration, actors were treated on almost the same level as the lowest class of pariahs, and *gesakusha* were classified together with clowns as "entertainers." Most of the actors and *gesakusha* themselves did not even question this treatment. Even after the Restoration, Kanagaki Robun would refer to himself as a "base person of a lowly occupation," as has already been mentioned. Nevertheless, until around 1886, this same Kanagaki Robun "continue to wield supreme power over the *gesaku* world. Anyone wishing to be a novelist had to go to him, pay him the customary entrance fees, and become his disciple. In exchange, the would-be novelist would be given a pen name containing either the character *Ro* or the character *Bun* from the master's name. Literary success could never be hoped for unless this procedure was followed." (Ichijima Shunjô)

Therefore, in a period when "to have graduated from a university was a passport to all honors and success, which were beckoning before every college graduate," to reject "these beckonings of worldly success and to plunge into a calling of a low social position," as Kôda Rohan put it, was more effective than a hundred arguments in breaking down the social prejudices against the novel. In this way, Tsubouchi's assertion that the novel was an art form was backed up by his actions and succeeded in convincing many young men.

In his biography of Futabatei Shimei *(Futabatei Shimei no Isshô),* Uchida Roan tells us that *Shôsetsu Shinzui* and *Tôsei Shosei Katagi* completely changed the public's thinking about the novel. "From the lowly status of the *gesaku,* the novel at one leap was transformed into a vital element contributing to civilization, into a respectable occupation which even prominent scholars were not ashamed to regard as their mission. The young men of the time, who until this time had thought that politics was the only possible way to realize their ambitions, now discovered this new world. Like sleepers who had been suddenly awakened, they all rushed towards literature. When Bimyô and Kôyô decided to devote their lives to literature, they were motivated by the success of Harunoya Oboro."

It was not only Yamada Bimyô and Ozaki Kôyô; Kôda Rohan and Futabatei Shimei also tried their hands at literature under the influence of Tsubouchi.

Thus, the effects of Tsubouchi's literary revolution were more far-reaching in its extraneous influence than in its contents. A secondary result of this idea that the novel is an art form was that Tsubouchi asserted the independence of fiction as an art form in opposition to the utilitarian viewpoint which sought to make use of novels for the purposes of ethical teaching or of political propaganda.

"That which is called art," wrote Tsubouchi, "is fundamentally not the same as the useful arts. Rather, its only object ought to be to delight the mind and to penetrate the subtlest depths of the soul."

This follows as a logical conclusion from the above-mentioned exaltation of the novel, and the distinction between the fine arts and the useful arts is based on one of the fundamental principles of Western aesthetics. Without such a conscious awareness of the independence of fiction, the modern novel could not possibly have developed in any country in the world, and it is quite clear that this was one of the major contents of the reform wrought by Tsubouchi.

Against the social background of the times, this idea of the independence of fiction was asserted, on one hand, in protest against the interference of traditional Confucianism with the subject matter of fiction. On the other hand, it was asserted in opposition to the utilitarianism of the new Englishment and its concrete manifestation, the political novel. While despising the gesaku literature, Confucianism had permitted the existence of these novels, "harmful to morals and to the minds of the people," only under the condition that they serve the purpose of en-

couraging virtue and chastising evil. This role of Confucianism evidently
appeared to Tsubouchi to be the greatest obstacle hindering the improvement and advancement of Japanese fiction, and it was for this reason that
he attacked the Confucian view of fiction as well as the literary style of
Kyokutei Bakin, the author of *Nansô Satomi hakkenden*, who catered
sevilely to it. Tsubouchi declares, first of all: "The chief matter of the
novel is human passions; this is followed by [depiction of] manners and
customs. . . . By human passions are meant the sensual desires of human
beings, what the Buddhists call the one hundred and eight appetites of
the flesh." He continues: "The task of the novelist is to penetrate to the
inmost depths of the human passions, to depict without omission the
hidden secrets in the hearts, not only of the so-called virtuous and manly,
but also of young and old, men and women, good and bad, and righteous
and unrighteous. In this way, scrupulously and meticulously, the novelist
must reveal the human passions in graphic, vivid form." He regrets that
the famous traditional novelists of China and Japan "stopped merely at
the superficial delineation of the human passions, which ought to be the
chief matter of the novel." If the novelist, he says, "produces by his own
contriving characters which go against the human passions, nay, which
contradict the known principles of human psychology, then such characters are not entities belonging to the real world of human beings, but
merely characters existing in the author's imagination. No matter how
skillful may be the depiction, no matter how striking and unusual the
plot, such writings ought not be called novels. . . . For instance, the eight
heroes of the *Hakkenden*, the masterpiece of Kyokutei Bakin, are nothing
but incarnations of the eight Confucian virtues, and can by no means be
called real human beings."

Here Tsubouchi advocates a consistent, thoroughgoing realism. The
fact that this advocacy of realism was not a mere theory for Tsubouchi,
but rather came as the product of Tsubouchi's own temperament, was
corroborated at a later date in the "No Ideals Controversy," a literary
dispute between Tsubouchi and Mori Ôgai. As a matter of fact, this advocacy of realism was the most effective weapon which could be used
to break down the traditional prejudices against the *gesaku* literature, and

also in view of its far-reaching influence on succeeding generations, it was this idea which formed the nucleus of *Shôsetsu Shinzui*.

At this point, the ideas expounded in *Shôsetsu Shinzui* assume a greater degree of concreteness and are expressed in the following formulation: "The novel is art. However, in order to be art, the novel must be realistic."

This concept is, of course, inseparably related with the above-mentioned idea of the autonomous value of art. For pure realism can have no other purpose but realism itself. To have any other objectives or aims would mean to distort realism. And it was also a logical necessity that this realization, which is a prerequisite for the establishment of modern fiction, should, in the contemporary social conditions, lead to an anti-utilitarian, anti-political attitude.

Tsubouchi's student days overlapped with the period of intensified political enthusiasm of 1881 and 1882, and many of his acquaintances were members of the radical political parties after their graduation. Nevertheless, Tsubouchi had an inborn indifference to politics.

The appearance and the success of *Shôsetsu Shinzui* and *Tôsei Shosei Katagi* signified the end of the period of politics in the novel. "The unheard-of popularity" of Tsubouchi's works, writes Uchida Roan, "came at a time when politics had gone into a period of quiescence with the announcement that the Government promised to establish a system of representative government within a few years; the mind of the people then turned to literature."

Tsubouchi himself, in the preface to the eleventh installment of *Tôsei Shosei Katagi,* replied to politically minded critics of his novel, who expressed the opinion that it was silly to engage in such worthless writing, ignoring the necessity of discussing politics. "It would be more worthwhile to translate political novels." In reply to these arguments, Tsubouchi answered: "This criticism is the fallacious statement of specialists in utilitarianism who equate the novel with the 'useful arts' and who desire to make art into a machine solely at the disposal of politicians. They, however, are ignorant of the true essence of the novel. . . . This amounts to nothing but petrified Confucian moralism. . . . They are merely people of the utilitarian school who look for fiction in politics."

Tsubouchi clearly perceived that Confucianism and Western-type utilitarianism both shared the common view of the novel and of "art." However, it should be noted that his rejection of these "specialists in utilitarianism" is far more scathing than his rejection of the *gesaku* literature of the past. This is related to the fact that his ideals have been regarded as being, in a sense, a revival of the thought of Motoori Norinaga, and also to the fact that the main current in the "new" literature which appeared after him was the fiction of the Kenyûsha, which was modeled after the literature of the Genroku period. It is interesting that the literary revolution wrought by this *bungakushi* was not aimed at modernizing the political novel, which was the literature of the intellectual class. Instead, it attempted to modernize literature on the basis of the traditional *gesaku* literature inherited from the Edo period. This fact had a considerable influence on the nature of modern Japanese fiction in the subsequent periods.

We may summarize in a nutshell the accomplishments of Tsubouchi by saying that he *rejected* the political novel and *improved* the *gesaku* literature. In temperament, Tsubouchi was a man of letters of the same type as Kanagaki Robun and Hattori Bushô.

In his preface to *Shôsetsu Shinzui*, Tsubouchi writes: "Ever since my youthful days I have enjoyed Japanese novels. For more than a decade, I have spent every available moment of my precious time in their perusal. As a result, I have attained considerable familiarity with both old and new Japanese novels." Ichijima Shunjô also attests that "even during his student days, Tsubouchi was already a fine novelist of the old school."

The goal at which Tsubouchi aimed was, therefore, to "improve" his beloved *gesaku* literature to the point where it would be worthy of the appreciation of the intellectual class. Although he may have derived his concept of fiction from the English novel, the concrete content of this "art form" did not go much farther than an idealized "improvement" of the old-style Japanese novels, in which Kyokutei Bakin would be made more realistic and Tamenaga Shunsui more noble.

Therefore, it was only to be expected that *Tôsei shosei katagi,* the concrete exemplification of this theory, was in essence an "improved *gesaku.*" It was also precisely for this reason that *Tôsei Shosei Katagi* could be accepted so readily by the general reading public.

This was a novel depicting in a light, whimsical vein the life of university students, who were, along with the jinrikisha, regarded as the symbols of the new era in contemporary Tokyo. As his models, Tsubouchi took his classmates at Tokyo University. The novel exposes in a suitable manner the seamy sides of pawnbrokers, vaudeville houses, the gay quarters, and beef restaurants. The book does not go to excesses, and since it depicts an environment in which the author himself lived, the living patterns of the students are presented in a vivid, albeit external manner. Thus, the novel did indeed have freshness.

However, the work retained very strongly the odor of the old literature. Not only was the literary style almost exactly that of the *gesaku* literature; the plot also followed the time-honored traditions of abandoned children, children of different parents switched by mistake, and reunions of long-lost brothers and sisters. The "human passions," of which the author had made so much mention, were merely depicted perfunctorily, and the characterization of the persons appearing in the story was nothing more than a "mixture of the eccentric and the mediocre," the characters having neither the breadth nor the thickness of real human beings, as Takada Sanae had already pointed out at the time.

Despite its apparently brilliant success, Tsubouchi's reform of the novel was unable, in the end, to attain a thoroughness or completeness in its concrete contents. That is, in his attempt to elevate the novel to the level of an art form, Tsubouchi succeeded only in producing a work as unartistic as *Tôsei shosei katagi.* He had to pay for this failure by his extraordinarily short lifetime as a novelist. In this consisted the true nature of the suffering which he was condemned to taste as a pioneer.

The literary concepts of the new era proposed by Tsubouchi rather vaguely in his *Shôsetsu Shinzui* and *Tôsei Shosei Katagi* had a dual nature. One aspect of them, the drive towards modernization, gave birth to the work of Futabatei Shimei and Yamada Bimyô. The other aspect, the revival of the *gesaku* literature of the Edo period, gave birth to the work of Ozaki Kôyô and Kôda Rohan. In this sense, Tsubouchi Shôyô is unmistakably the father of the modern Japanese novel. The appearance of both Futabatei Shimei and Ozaki Kôyô signified a further develop ment of the contradictions contained in the ideas expressed in *Shôsetsu Shinzui*. The development attained by both of these writers surpassed even the expectations of Tsubouchi, and they also transcended completely the limitations of his concepts of literature.

As a result, after the publication of *Saikun* (The Wife) in January, 1889, Tsubouchi Shôyô ceased to write fiction entirely. Thus, the author of *Shôsetsu shinzui* worked as a novelist for only slightly longer than four years.

CHAPTER IV

Ukigumo and Futabatei Shimei

Futabatei Shimei carried a little too far and hastily the literary movement started by Tsubouchi Shôyô to establish the novel as a legitimate branch of the literary arts. His point of view was too far advanced to be accepted generally at that time; and it was this unhappy circumstance that caused him to give up his literary activities later.

Like Shôyô, Futabatei was born to the family of a former samurai serving for the dukedom of Bishû (part of present-day Aichi Prefecture). He was born in Tokyo, which was then called "Edo." He first wished to follow his father in a military career; but, having failed to enter the Army Academy because of his near-sightedness, he changed his mind and entered Tokyo School of Foreign Languages, where he specialized in Russian with the hope of becoming a diplomat after graduation. Becoming more and more proficient in the language, however, he took an ever greater interest in the study of Russian literature, which influenced him so much that it is even said to have shaped his character.

In those days, he does not seem to have had a strong desire to enter the literary profession. But, about the time when the publication of *Shôsetsu Shinzui* (The Essence of the Novel) and *Tôsei Shosei Katagi* (The Character of the Modern Student) indicated a rise of a new literature, incident happened which led to his leaving school. Tokyo School of Foreign Languages was abolished as a result of the reformation of the school system and he was to be transferred to another school, where he did not wish to study at all. He gave up school and made up his mind to try his fortune in the literary world. It was at this juncture in his life that he paid his first visit to Tsubouchi Shôyô. This visit marked the commencement of his literary career as well as the beginning of their lifelong friendship.

Shôyô in later years recollected, "I first got acquainted with Futabatei in January, 1886. At that time, he was probably the foremost authority on Russian literature in Japan. In the field of literary criticism he seemed to admire Belinsky, and among the writers he seemed particularly to admire Pushkin, Lermontov, Turgenev and Goncharov." At their first interview, it is said, Futabatei was bold enough to ask Shôyô some questions about those points in *Shôsetsu Shinzui* which seemed dubious to him in the light of what he had acquired from his study of Russian literature.

On the other hand, Shôyô had such an insight and modesty as to acknowledge the uncommon talent of young Futabatei, whom he had just met. Shôyô had of course read the classics while in college, but his post-school literary study had been limited to Scott, Lytton, Dickens, Dumas and a few other authors. Thus, he confessed, "From Futabatei I learned for the first time about an entirely different literary theory and I discovered in him a very unique sort of character that I had never expected to meet among us Japanese. It was the peculiarity of his character rather than the novelty of his literary theory that surprised me." Shôyô, describing Futabatei as the Rousseau of Japan, admitted, though not overtly, that Futabatei far surpassed him not only as a thinker but also as a literary man in the new age. He goes on to say, "We were very dissimilar in character, while in taste we had much in common. This happy coincidence seems to have had much to do with the intimacy of our friendship. In contrast with his character, attitude and opinion, my own defects seemed to become so clear to me that I felt the urgent need to improve myself." Shôyô made this humble confession at the age of 27 or 28, when he had every reason to regard himself as a great literary success. It is true that this fact suggests his straightforwardness and modesty rather than Futabatei's remarkable talent. But it seems also to imply the immeasurable impressiveness and peculiarity of Futabatei's character, which, as Shôyô says, was of a "sort never to be found among the entire Japanese people." The impact of such a peculiar character upon Shôyô was so tremendous as to lead even Shôyô, who had strong self-confidence and self-esteem, to the "realization of the impropriety of his attitude" and also to the "spontaneous reflection upon his insincerity in literary work and frivority in conduct of life."

In view of the profound influence of Russian literature on the formation of Futabatei's character, we have to look at the particular circumstances under which he studied Russian at Tokyo School of Foreign Languages. The Russian Department of the School had originated as a part of the Institute for the Training of the Official Interpreters founded during the Tokugawa feudal regime. At the School some of the students were granted scholarships. At the Russian Department, most of the instructors were Russians, and the courses offered were almost the same as those taught in Russian secondary schools. All the subjects, ranging from physics, chemistry and mathematics to rhetric and the history of Russian literature, were taught in Russian. Such being the case, the Department seemed as if it were a school in a Russian colony.

In the advanced courses, as some of Futabatei's classmates recollect, the unavailability of suitable textbooks created the expedient and peculiar type of instruction: during each period, the students just listened to their teacher read aloud a novel or a drama, and after the reading of each work they were required to submit their papers written in Russian about their personal criticism on each of the characters in the work.

The instructor who did most of this reading was a Russian American named Gray. He was a liberalist refugee; but he had a deep interest in literature and was quite skilled in reading aloud. His vivid reading, often accompanied by realistic gestures (especially in his reading of dramas), fascinated his students. It is said that they took as much delight in his reading of Russian novels as they did in the reading of Japanese novels. Here it has to be noted that this expedient means of instruction resulted, though quite unexpectedly, in laying much the soundest foundation for the proper appreciation of foreign literary works.

In bringing forth this excellent result, there are at least two noteworthy factors. In the first place, the students did not read printed Russian letters but concentrated on listening, without the aid of written materials, to the language as read aloud by a native speaker. This instruction, which has much in common with the reading in the *salon,* enabled the students to cultivate the aesthetic appreciation of the sounds of language, which Japanese literary men have found to be the most difficult element to comprehend in their study of modern European literature.

In this connection, Futabatei states, "Silent reading does not enable us to perceive any beauty inherent in European languages. On the other hand, reading aloud, if properly and appreciatively performed, will reveal the beauty of their rhythms and tones. European languages are musical. Their tones are so pleasant and musical that we can find pleasure even in mere listening to a man or woman read aloud some passages in an European language." ("My Criteria for Translation"). This is an excellent remark and is also suggestive of the profundity of Gray's influence upon Futabatei.

In the second place, since the students had no particular desire to follow the literary profession, they could afford to take a genuinely humanistic interest in fictional characters and concentrate on grasping the contents, without having their attention diverted to the minute study of formal literary techniques exemplified in the foreign novels. Moreover, their repeated exercises in personal criticism on the characters trained the students, with the result that they obtained a deep and clear insight into both the moral and the social problems represented in the novels they studied.

This is, needless to say, the most natural and ideal manner of cultivating the proper appreciation of novels, vernacular or foreign. Unfortunately, however, most of the Japanese writers in the Meiji era failed to develop facility in literary appreciation, even through they read Tolstoi or Maupassant in the original.

The instruction which Futabatei had received at Tokyo School of Foreign Languages gave him such a remarkable reading ability as to enable him to read and appreciate Russian novels with almost the same precision as a native Russian. He took a keen interest in the social problems represented in the novels he read, and it was a natural consequence that he devoured the critical essays by Belinsky or Herzen. Besides, Futabatei was deeply concerned with the incomprehensible problems of life. In view of these circumstances, it seems quite natural that he should have come to be regarded as the rare Japanese author impersonating the pessimistic and ponderous traits of the Slavic character.

On one hand, the uniqueness of his character and literary attainments underlay his epoch-marking novelty exemplified in *Ukigumo* (The Floating Cloud), *Aibiki* (Rendez-vous), and *Meguriai* (Chance Meeting). *Ukigumo* is one of his masterpieces, which he wrote with all the ardor of his youth. On the other hand, his uniqueness was evidently responsible for his isolated and unhappy position in the literary world of Japan, in which he always regarded himself as a literary outlaw. From our modern point of view, however, he is a most respectable man of letters. His literary ability, which derived from his study of Russian literature, was then considered as peculiar and exceptional. But his abilities were in fact pervaded with a far more natural and humanistic spirit than the other Japanese literary men in the Meiji era acquired through their study of foreign literature. It is this particularly innovating and modernizing aspect of Futabatei's literary traits that has established his novels as the first instances of true modernism in Japanese literature. Making them, of course, distinctly worthy of our careful analysis in the present time—though their merits were not recognized during his lifetime.

Ukigumo is an unfinished novel which Futabatei wrote under Shôyô's guidance during the four years (1886–9). Book One and Book Two of the novel were published separately in book form under the name of Tsubouchi Shôyô; the former in June of 1887 and the latter in February of the next year. Book Three was published serially in the magazine, *Miyako no Hana* (The Flower of the Metropolis), Nos. 18–20, 1889. About that time, Futabatei was studying the critical essays by Belinsky and some other critics, and this led him, as he says, to "write *Ukigumo* with the serious intention of depicting, in a revealing and critical manner, the inside of the civilized society of Japan." In *Ukigumo* he tries to put forward his criticism of Japanese society by means of comparing the two chief characters: an honest but irresolute and poor idealist named Bunzô Utsumi and a mean and shrewd fame-seeker named Noboru Honda. They used to be fellow officials in a government office. Bunzô was disinclined to curry favor with his senior officials, and in the course of time he was thrown out of office. This incident involved the Sonoda's family, who were relatives of Bunzô and also were well acquainted with Noboru. At that time Bunzô was living with the Sonodas. Sonoda's only daughter Osei had been so intimate with Bunzô from their childhood as to be looked upon as his fiancee. After Bunzô lost his job, however, she grew disillusioned, mainly because of his irresoluteness and self-contempt, due to his poverty. She began to take a fancy to Noboru, who was more cheerful and affable. To Bunzô she had become so indifferent as to refuse to speak a word to him, even though they were still living in the same house. After a series of troubles and complications, Osei finally gave herself to Noboru. On the other hand, Bunzô's love for Osei cooled off a little. Nevertheless, when she got into difficulty, Bunzô, from compassion, endeavored to help her out of the difficulty, only to fail in his effort. This failure drove him to despair and finally into insanity.

The conclusion of this novel has remained unwritten, and we only know that the author had a few plans, which differed from each other in minor points.

Futabatei states that by Bunzô he tried to "represent exaggeratingly certain traits of his own character." Bunzô, who is very similar to Futabatei in character, is in a sense his caricature and may probably be the ideal type of man he conceived. Bunzô can thus be looked upon as the pure embodiment of the ideas that Futabatei cherished at that time. Probably, Futabatei himself wished to obtain worldly success and happiness, which he symbolized by Osei in *Ukigumo*. He was made to realize, however, that in the stern realities of Meiji society, mere idealism and honest character would be no qualification for success in life. Thus, in *Ukigumo* he had to make the plot in which success, which Bunzô wished for, was to be yielded up to Noboru, a mean but shrewd fellow full of vitality.

Futabatei says, "I myself thought that it would be persons like Noboru that were numerous and were to be prosperous and also powerful in the modern society of Japan."

This accounts for the circumstance that *Ukigumo* seems to be an expression of the author's own self-contempt. His ideas as exemplified by the ethical contrast between Bunzô and Noboru were long cherished and developed in his mind, until it found its expression in his later works, *Sono Omokage* (The Image) and *Chasen-gami* (Tea-Whisk Coiffure). In each of these novels, the central character is depicted as being of the same unheroic type as Bunzô, with meager adaptability to life. This defective quality Futabatei regarded as a sort of mental deformity. Here seems to lie the essential point of his criticism on the Meiji intelligentsia. *Ukigumo,* though somewhat comic in form, distinctly brings forth the most serious problem of the inner life of Meiji people, i.e., the absolute separation of the criteria for material life from those for moral life. This problem is presented in the form of the sharp contrast between the ignorance on the part of the intelligentsia about how to get along in the realities of life and the prosperity enjoyed by the untrustworthy but very adaptable people.

This was the same sort of probelm considered seriously by Sôseki and Ôgai; and it is still a problem confronting us at the present time. It is true that *Ukigumo* was in a sense an outcome of the profound influence exerted upon Futabatei by such Russian authors as Belinsky, Turgenev, and particularly Goncharov. (It is Futabatei's own affirmation that *Ukigumo* was written by applying the principal ideas in Goncharov's *Precipice* to the situation in Japan.) But it is a far more significant fact, which does much credit to modern Japanese novel literature as well as to Futabatei himself, that *Ukigumo,* which has been regarded as the first modern Japanese novel, was written on the basis of a keen and deep insight into the realities of Japanese society.

However, Futabatei's unprecedented modernism hardly received any recognition in the literary world at that time. It was merely the novelty of his style and the accuracy of his description that attracted attention. (To make the description realistic, he wrote *Ukigumo* in the colloquial language, instead of in a flowerly literary style, as had been the tradition. Thus, Futabatei, together with Yamada Bimyo, has been regarded as the first Japanese novelist that wrote in a colloquial style.)

It was also due to his use of colloquial style and accurate description that he was respected by the naturalist writers twenty years later as their predecessor. Futabatei introduced the essentials of modern novel literature into Japan, laying the excellent foundation for true modernism in Japanese novel literature. This is his greatest achievement, and is ever to be remembered in the history of the Japanese novel. However, it was his very modernity that made his isolation in the literary world inevitable. His too progressive ideas were responsible for his tragic literary career.

Besides *Ukigumo,* he wrote two novels, *Sono Omokage* (The Image) and *Heibon* (Mediocrity), after twenty years of silence. They are fairly good novels with some merits of their own, but they have no particular literary significance.

It must also be remembered that Futabatei was an excellent translator. His translations of works by Turgenev, Gogol, Gorky, Andreyev, Garshin and some other writers exerted a remarkable and inspiring influence upon the writers of the Meiji era. Among his translations we have to take special notice of *Aibiki* (Rendez-vous) and *Meguriai* (Chance Meeting). The former is a translation of a chapter in Turgenev's *A Sportsman's Sketches* and the latter a translation of the same author's *Three Encounters,* a medium-length work based on data collected during his journey through Italy. Like his own novels, Futabatei's translations were all written in colloquial Japanese. Instead of making free translation—most of the Japanese versions of foreign literary works had been very liberal translations—he endeavored to make very careful literal translations to preserve the poetic flavor of the original works. His translations, thus justly regarded as literary works worth serious aesthetic study, evoked the great admiration of the literary world. They made a far more refreshing impression than *Ukigumo,* upon the younger writers such as Tôson, Doppo, Katai, Roka, and some others.

Futabatei also translated Turgenev's *Parasha* and *Rudin;* the former being published in 1896 under the Japanese title *Katakoi* (Unreturned

Love), and the latter in 1897 under the title *Ukikusa* (The Floating Weed). Besides these, his translations of Andreyev's *The Red Laugh* (1908) and some of Gorky's works are noteworthy literary achievements.

CHAPTER V

<

Kenyûsha

Shôyô and Futabatei, who had been active leaders in the literary reform movement, gave up their novel-writing after the 22nd year of
Meiji (1889). This was the tragedy of their literary lines. It may be seen
that it was the subtle shifting of the social conditions of the times which
was largely responsible for their abandonment of the novel as their form
of expression.

The process of Japan's westernization (in the sense of 'modernization'),
having started at the time of the Restoration, reached its climax about the
20th year of Meiji, when the *Rokumeikan* and its superficial westernization were in vogue. However, due to the shallowness of its imitation of
Occidentalism, the westernizing movement came to be the target for
severe criticism and attack from the general public. In addition, the unsuccessful attempt of the Japanese Government to revise the unequal
provisions of the treaties with foreign powers gave rise to strong dissatisfaction among the Japanese people. These two factors combined in
bringing about the rise of an excessive nationalism, a movement unprecedented in the previous twenty years. It was a reaction against the
hitherto prevailing Occidentalizing trends.

In 1888, Miyake Setsurei, Shiga Jûkô, and Sugiura Jûgô organized the
Seikyôsha (Society for Political Enlightenment). Their opinions were
propagated chiefly by means of the organization's magazine, *Nip, o i-jin*
(The Japanese). Not only did it advocate the conservative principles of
national rights but it also emphasized the necessity and importance of
preserving Japan's ancient art works and of restoring genuine Japanese

literature. Their propaganda led public opinion toward a stronger nationalism.

This rise of nationalism was in a sense an inevitable step for Japan in its drive for modernization. She was making every effort to catch up with the more advanced Western powers by developing her capitalistic economic system. And, as the history of Europe suggests, the concepts of national rights and national consciousness are essential factors in organizing a truly modern state. Japan had been trying to import capitalism from Europe and America as the most effective means of modernizing herself. After twenty years of such blind imitation of Occidentalism, however, the Japanese people began to develop a more matured conception of modern civilization. At such a stage in the modernization process it is quite natural that they should have developed a strong national consciousness; and it can even be said that this strong nationalistic movement among the Japanese was a sign of their maturing as an integrated nation, marking in a sense the completion of their imitation of European countries. Besides, it is a noteworthy fact that this nationalistic movement was coming into being about the same time in which Japan's modern industries, particularly her light industries, were making rapid growth and the reins of her still clan oriented government were becoming stabilized through the promulgation of the Constitution of 1889 and the inauguration of the Diet.

Under these circumstances, it may reasonably be said that the advocacy of nationalism fulfilled a need which grew out of the social tendencies of the times. Moreover, its supporters, entirely different from the previous simple-minded reactionaries, had received a modern European type of education and yet found themselves dissatisfied with the then prevalent occidentalizing trends. They were serious thinkers whose knowledge and insights were profound enough to lead the public opinion of the times, and whose influence penetrated into every sphere of cultural activities.

In the sphere of novel literature, this nationalistic movement manifested itself in the form of a literary renaissance, shown particularly in the rediscovery of the merits of Saikaku (1642–1693); to this literary renaissance was closely related a decline in the use of colloquial style in literary works. Of course, this resulted in a great loss in popularity for Shôyô, Futabatei, Bimyô and some other progressive novelists. They were replaced by another group of writers represented by Ozaki Kôyô and Kôda Rohan, both of whom preserved some of the literary traits of the Genroku era. Ozaki Kôyô headed the Kenyûsha (Literary Circle Sharing the Same Inkstone). This group's sudden rise and prosperity was one of the most remarkable events in the shifting trends of the literary world.

)The nationalistic movement, which had much to do with the rise of the Kenyûsha, was a reaction against the immaturity and superficiality of the nation-wide imitation of Occidentalism; and, in spite of its reactionary appearance, it was actually a natural outcome of the national consciousness which the Japanese people were developing in their effort to establish their nation as a modernized (capitalistic) state. In a somewhat analogous way, the Kenyûsha's literary movement originated as a reaction to the failing literary reform movement of Shôyô and Futabatei. Their movement had proved unsuccessful due to the immaturity of the modernizing process of the nation at large and also to immaturity in the reform movement itself. The literary activity of the Kenyûsha was, on one hand, a denial of the kind of modernism advocated by Shôyô and Futabatei, while on the other hand it accelerated in its own way the modernization of Japanese literature.

The rise of the Kenyûsha signified a renaissance of the type of literature which had prospered during the Tokugawa period. At the same time, however, we should notice that the novels by the members of the Kenyûsha were based on some of the modern principles of literature advocated by Shôyô; namely, that literature is a self-contained cultural activity independent of anything else, and that artistic activity, including literature, must not be motivated by any gain-seeking desire. Thus, it is not be too much to say that, Shôyô was obliged to give up his literary activity by the rise of a new literary trend, which in a way realized some of the very ideals that he had strongly advocated.

Shôyô made much of realistic description as one of the essentials of modern novel-writing. This principle had already been developed by

Saikaku, one of the greatest fiction writers of the Genroku era. It was Kôyô and Rohan who discovered this merit of Saikaku and mastered his style, ideas, and plot-developing techniques, and used them examples which they attempted to follow. These were the main reasons for their literary success.

The type of literature which succeeded during the brilliant Genroku era (1688–1704) was the fruit of the outbursting free spirit of the common people, who had been delivered from the authority of the Buddhistic dogmas prevalent since the Middle Ages, and who had not yet been brought under the oppressive influence of the Confucianism of the Early Modern Times. Thus, Genroku literature was the literature of the common people and as such has occupied a unique position in the literary history of Japan. It is quite understandable, therefore, that Genroku literature, possessing this unique character, should have come to be appreciated and respected again during the Meiji era, when the common people were delivered from the suppression of the feudal regime. The works of Saikaku were superior to those of Bakin or Tanehiko as realistic novels. This quality of Saikaku's works derived from his realism, and realism had much to do, also, with the superiority of Kôyô and Rohan, who, by following Saikaku's example, surpassed Shôyô and Futabatei. In addition, realism in the works of Kôyô and Rohan impressed their contemporary reading public as an innovation.

It is true that the innovative aspect of their works mainly lay in external appearances; yet there is no denying that they did produce a number of truly innovative elements. This was recognized by general readers and critics. Even Shôyô and Futabatei had to admit that, compared with Kôyô and Rohan, they were no longer innovators; this was the principle reason for their abandonment of novel-writing.

The literary activity of the Kenyûsha is now regarded by many as too old-fashioned and as a mere continuation of the literary tradition of the Tokugawa period. In its beginning, however, the Kenyûsha started as a literary circle composed of young students about twenty years of age, who had had no connection whatsoever with the previously popular low-class (cheap) novelists. In a sense, the Kenyûsha's literary movement arose in response to Shôyô's advocation of realism, and as a movement motivated by the idealistic desire to establish novel literature as a legitimate branch of art. It was this new and unique character that attracted attention to the Kenyûsha's literary activity.

To the literature of the Kenyûsha, Kunikida Doppo gave the nickname Japanese literature dressed in European style; this seems to be a most adequate description of the characteristic literary works by the members of the Kenyûsha.

The members of the Kenyûsha started their magazine *Garakuta-bunko* (Trash Library) in 1885, when leading members, such as Ozaki Kôyô, Yamada Bimyô, and Ishibashi Shian, were still students of the Preparatory School for the Tokyo Imperial university. *Garakuta-bunko* was at first a literary coterie magazine circulated only among the organization's members; but later it came to be printed and at the height of its prosperity no less than 3,000 copies were printed. Soon, however, it began to decline. In 1888, Bimyô, one of the most important leaders, seceded from Kenyûsha to become the editor of *Miyako no Hana* (The Flower of the Metropolis) published by Kinkôdô, one of the major publishing companies of the day. *Miyako no Hana* was highly respectable and prosperous, and was nicknamed 'The Queen of Novel Magazines'. This magazine soon outrivaled *Garakuta-bunko,* which ceased publication in the following year.

Yamada Bimyô was born in Tokyo in 1868. He was a friend of Kôyô and Futabatei from their boyhood. While a student of the Preparatory School for the Tokyo Imperial University he was already one of the leading figures of the Kenyûsha and was also a confidential comrade of Kôyô. In course of time, Bimyô came under the influence of English literature, particularly Chaucer and Shakespeare. In November of 1884, he began the serial publication of a historical novel *Musashi-no* (The Musashi Plain) in the *Yomiuri Newspaper*. His unique colloquial style in this novel was highly praised by the reading public. Following this success he published a number of novels and reviews in *Jogaku-zasshi* (The ~and in Kokumin no tomo~ Friends of the Nation). Such excellent and vigorous literary activity gained for him a reputation and fame almost as great as that of Shôyô, though he was still quite young. Of course, this had much to do with his being invited to become the editor-in-chief of *Miyako no Hana*, the most prosperous literary magazine of that time.

However, Bimyô's creative capacity was soon exhausted. His *Hana-guruma* (Flower Cart) serially published in the newly started *Miyako no Hana* was a poor work even to the eye of the readers of that day. *Hana-guruma* was his first rather labored work depicting his contemporary society. Then his historical novel, *Kochô* (Butterfly), published in *Koku-min no Tomo* in January of 1890, attracted some attention, partly by virtue of the nude pictures utilized as its illustrations. His later works *Ichigo-hime* (The Princess of Strawberries) and *Kabuto-giku* (Monk's-Helmet), both of which are historical novels, and *Kyôshi-zanmai* (Absorption in the Job of Teaching) and *Haku-gyoku-ran* (White-Ball-Orchid) were all relatively poor works. Thus, since he was unable to keep up with the new trends in novel literature created by Kôyô, Rohan, and Ôgai, Bimyô suspended his novel-writing after 1892. He then applied himself to the composition of new-style poems and to the formulation of his theory about this literary genre. In the genre of new-style poetry, Bimyô had already in 1889 published *Shin-tai Shi Sen* (An Anthology of New-Style Poems); and then in 1891 and 1892, he published serially in *Kokumin no Tomo* his theoretical work entitled *Nippon In-bun Ron* (On the Prosody of Japanese Poems). This latter work was the first serious prosodical study of the new-style poetry of Japan. This study, brought forth a refutation from Ôgai and Roan, which marked the beginning of the full-scale study of Japanese poetry. Bimyô studied various types and combinations of rhythms and metres, utilizing them in the composition of his own poems and in his translation of foreign poems. His poems and translations appeared in *Kokumin no Tomo* and elsewhere, and in 1892, he published an anthology entitled *Shin-chô In-bun Seinen Shôka-shû* (An Anthology of New-Style Poems for the Young). These poetical works and prosodical studies were after all only suggestive of the new forms of expression, which did not always gain success. Besides, Bimyô himself did not have the modern poetic sentiment necessary to

PLATE I

TAKAHASHI
ODEN YASHA
MONOGATARI
THE CAREER
OF A
CELEBRATED
MURDERESS)

KANAGAKI
ROBUN
(1929–94)

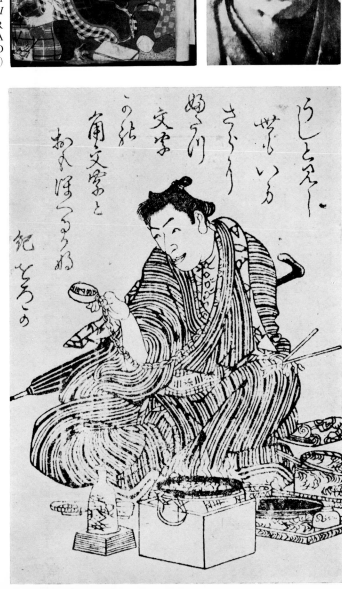

ILLUSTRATION TO THE *AGURANABE*

PLATE II

NARUSHIMA RYÛHOKU (1837–84)

PREFACE OF THE *RYÛKYÔ SHINSHI*
(NEW DESCRIPTION OF YANAGIBASHI)

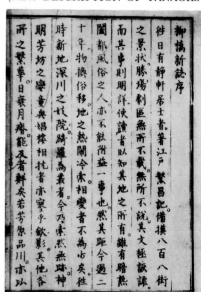

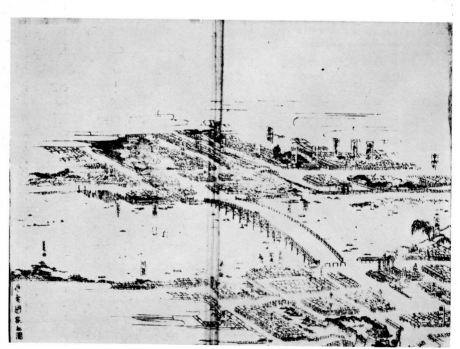

ILLUSTRATION TO THE *RYÛKYÔ SHINSHI*

PLATE III

NAKAMURA MASANAO
(KEIU) (1832–91)

FUKUZAWA YUKICHI
(1834–1901)

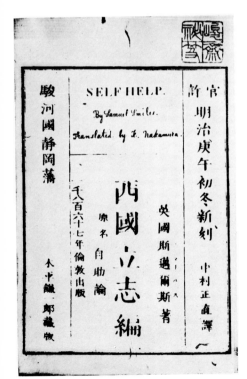

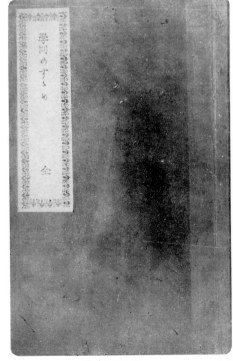

SAIKOKU RISSHI HEN
(SKETCHES OF SELF-MADE MEN
OF THE WEST) TRANSLATION
OF SAMUEL SMILES' *SELF-HELP*

GAKUMON NO SUSUME
(THE ENCOURAGEMENT OF LEARNING)

PLATE IV

YANO RYÛKEI (FUMIO)
(1850–1931)

KEIKOKU BIDAN
(LAUDABLE ANECDOTES OF
ABLE STATESMANSHIP)

ILLUSTRATION TO THE *KEIKOKU BIDAN*

PLATE V

TÔKAI SANSHI (SHIBA SHIRÔ) (1852–1922)

N NO KIGÛ
ANGE ENCOUNTERS
H BEAUTIFUL WOMEN)

ILLUSTRATION TO THE
KAJIN NO KIGÛ

KAKAN NO UGUISU (NIGHTINGALE AMID

PLATE VI

KARYÛ SHUNWA (A SPRING TALE OF FLOWERS AND WILLOWS): THE JAPANESE VERSION OF LYTTON'S *ERENEST MALTRAVERS*. TRANSLATION OF NIWA (ODA) JUNICHIRÔ (1851–1919)

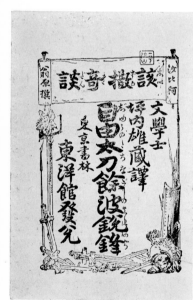

JIYÛ NO TACHI NAGORI NO KIREAJI (REMAINING SHARPNESS OF THE SWORD OF FREEDOM): TRANSLATION OF SHAKESPEARE'S *JULIUS CEASAR* BY TSUBOUCHI SHÔYÔ.

PLATE VII

SUBOUCHI SHÔYÔ
(ARUNOYA OBORO) (1859–1934)

TÔSEI SHOSEI KATAGI (CHARACTER
OF MODERN STUDENTS)

SHÔSETSU SHINZUI (THE ESSENCE
OF THE NOVEL)

ILLUSTRATION TO THE *TÔSEI SHOSEI KATAGI*

PLATE VIII

UKIGUMO (THE FLOATING CLOUDS)

FUTABATEI SHIMEI (1864–1909)

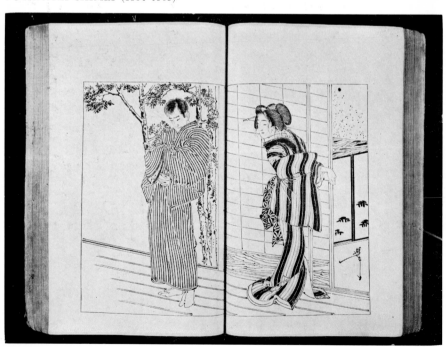

ILLUSTRATION TO THE *UKIGUMO*

PLATE IX

GARAKUTA BUNKO (TRASH LIBRARY)
—THE LITERARY COTERIE
MAGAZINE OF THE KENYÛSHA

OZAKI KÔYÔ (1867–1903)

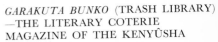

KONJIKI
YASHA
(A DEMON
OF GOLD)

ILLUSTRATION TO THE *KONJIKI YASHA*

PLATE X

YAMADA BIMYÔ (1868–1910)   KÔDA ROHAN (1867–1947)

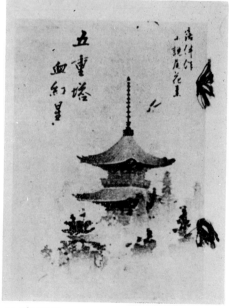

ILLUSTRATION TO THE *KOCHÔ*
(BUTTERFLY)

GOJÛNOTÔ
(A FIVE-STORIED PAGODA)

PLATE XI

MORI ÔGAI (1862–1922)

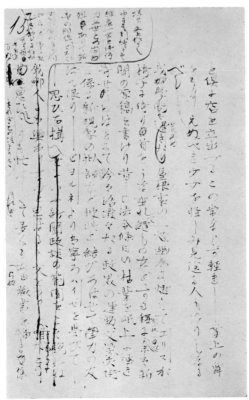

ÔGAI'S MANUSCRIPT OF THE *MAIHIME*
(THE DANCING GIRL)

PLATE XII

THE STAFF OF THE *BUNGAKU KAI*
From the left of the front row. Ueda Bin, Hoshino
Tenchi, Togawa Shûkotsu, Hoshino Yûkage.
From the left of the rear, Shimazaki Tôson, Baba
Kochô, Hirata Tokuboku.

KITAMURA TÔKOKU (1868–94)

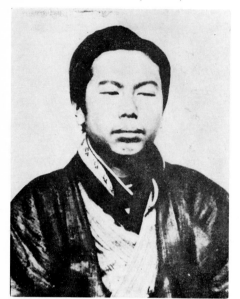

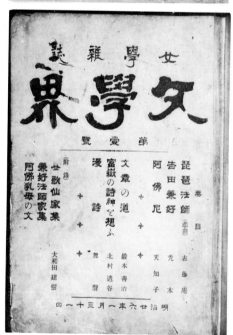

HÔRAIKYOKU (THE SONG OF
MT. HÔRAI, AN ANTHOLOGY)

THE MAGAZINE *"BUNGAKU KAI"*

PLATE XIII

GUCHI ICHIYÔ (1872-92)

PICTURE SCROLL OF
ICHIYÔ'S *NIGORIE*
(MUDDY STREAM),
PAINTED BY KABURAKI
KIYOKATA

MANUSCRIPT OF THE *TAKE
KURABE* (COMPARING HEIGHTS)

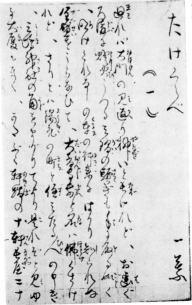

PLATE XIV

IZUMI KYÔKA (1873–1939)

FÛRYÛSEN (RAILWAY
LINE OF ROMANCE)

ILLUSTRATION TO THE KÔYA HIJIRI (TRAVELLING MONK)

PLATE XV

KAWAKAMI BIZAN
(1869–1908)

HIROTSU RYÛRÔ
(1861–1928)

KOSUGI TENGAI
(1865–1952)

PLATE XVI

TOKUTOMI ROKA (KENJIRÔ)
(1868–1927)

ROKA AND TOLSTOI IN YASNAYA POLYANA IN
1906

KINOSHITA NAOE (1869–1937)

A STAGE SCENE FROM THE PERFORMANCE OF
ROKA'S *HOTOTOGISU* (THE CUCKOO)

PLATE XVII

KUNIKIDA DOPPO
(1871–1908)

MUSAHINO
(MUSASHI PLAIN)

國木田獨步著

武藏堅

東京 民友社 發兌

ILLUSTRATION TO THE
AZAMUKAZARU NO KI
(AN HONEST RECORD)

PLATE XVIII

TAYAMA KATAI (1871–1930)

ILLUSTRATION TO THE *INAKA KYÔSHI* (COUNTRY TEACHER)

FUTON (BEDDING), PUBLISHED IN THE MAGAZINE *SHINSHÔSETSU*

PLATE XIX

SHIMAZAKI TOSON (1872–1943)

WAKANA SHÛ
(YOUNG HERBS:
A COLLECTION OF POEMS)

ILLUSTRATION TO THE *HAKAI*
(BREAKING AN OATH)

PLATE XX

TOKUDA SHUSEI (1871–1943)   MASAMUNE HAKUCHÔ (1879–1962)

IWANO HOMEI (1873–1920)

create the modern poetic forms that he advocated. Lacking the proper poetic sentiment, he simply did not possess in him the makings of a successful poet. A few years later, he made his temporary 'comeback' by publishing several realistic novels, including *Ochiyo*, 1896, and *Karenkyô*, 1898. After that, however, his works did not find much public favor; for example, his historical novels written in his later years, such as *Jirô Tsunetaka*, 1908, and *Taira no Shigehira*, 1910, failed to win the appraisal due their quality. Thus, in his later years, Bimyô was unhappy and unsuccessful as a writer, and died in 1911. His contemporary Iwaki Juntarô, commenting on him, says, 'Indeed, Bimyô had an excellent power of expression. However, it is a matter for regret that he lacked in the sympathy, sensibility, or enthusiasm that are required from a man of letters. Such being the case, his more incisive arguments seem, ironically enough, to reveal more sharply the superficial nature of his surveys. The more skilful techniques he displays in his description, the less impressive it sounds to his readers.' This statement seems to be representative of the opinion of his contemporaries. However, this kind of comment on his literary ability and the defects in his character does not produce a fair evaluation of his achievement, for it is merely based on the consequence of his literary activities. It might be much fairer to say that Bimyô, like his contemporary writers Shôyô and Futabatei, was simply a victim of the rapidly changing literary and intellectual currents of the times.

It is true that none of Bimyô's works in poetry, criticism, poetic theory, or any other genre has remained as a permanently valuable literary achievement. In his own time, however, he did perform a fairly significant role in the fields of literature with which he concerned himself.

Futabatei also was destined to be an unappreciated and tragic literary pioneer, but it was because he was too much in advance of his contemporaries; whereas Bimyô was a literary failure because of his excessive adaptability in changing with the current of the times.

In short, as Uchida Roan puts it, Bimyô was a 'premature child of the enthusiastic Occidentalizing trends of those times.' It may also be said that he was an all-round man, who proved to be a literary failure. His literary career symbolizes some of the characteristic aspects of the Kenyûsha's literature, often described as 'Japanese literature dressed in European style.'

What enabled the Kenyûsha literary movement to achieve something worth while and produce certain accomplished works was the literary talent and systematic effort of Ozaki Kôyô. Unlike Bimyô, who was a Jack-of-all-trades, Ozaki Kôyô devoted the 37 years of his life almost exclusively to the writing of novels, showing almost no interest in anything else, except the composition of *haiku* poems as his pastime. Due to such intense application, he was considered the greatest novelist of Japan when he died in 1903. His death was an event of great importance in the literary history of the Meiji era; it marked the end of the popularity of the type of literature advocated by the Kenyûsha, and its replacement by more naturalistic literature.

Ozaki Kôyô was born in Tokyo in 1867. He was, as mentioned earlier, a leader of the Kenyûsha from his student days. In April, of 1890, he published the medium-sized novel *Ni-nin Bikuni Iro-zange* (The Confession of Love Affairs by Two Nuns), which by winning for him a greater literary reputation than Bimyô, established him as the most popular writer of that time. The content of this novel was not particularly new, and its success was mainly due to its innovative style. 'Kôyô's peculiar style,' says Iwaki Juntarô, 'was neither a compromise between highly literary and vulgar styles, nor was it colloquialism. It was the product of his endeavor to master the brevity and feeling exemplified in the *haibun* (the type of literature expressing by means of prose style such spirit and feelings as are most typically conveyed by *haiku*) by Saikaku and Yayû, whom he studied and looked up to as his models. It was in his attempt to compete with Bimyô that Kôyô applied himself to the study of *haibun*.

Kôyô's *Ni-nin Bikuni Iro-zange* was often compared with Bimyô's *Kochô,* and it was even said that the former might be a better work than the latter. Partly because of this, 1890 was an epoch-marking year in the literary history of Meiji. This year marked the commencement of the competition between Kôyô and Bimyô and also the rise of the Kenyûsha.

The success of *Iro-zange* determined Kôyô's later literary career and in a broader sense it determined the tendencies and characteristics of the novels to be written by members of the Kenyûsha. As it is often said, the kind of art that is best accepted in a period is the one that is in advance of the period not by one step but by a half step. In this sense, Kôyô's novels had in all their respects just such a degree of innovation, that is, his works were half a step in advance of the times in which he lived.

As for the novelty of his style, it did not come strictly from innovative ideas, as in the case of Futabatei, but was deliberately molded through Kôyô's painstaking self-training and close comparative study of various styles. Writing in such a style, he employed every possible technique to satisfy his contemporaries' sense of beauty. His style indicates that he was the first to break away from the tradition of the Bunka and the Bunsei writers, which had been largely unconsciously copied to the time of Shôyô and Futabatei (Shôyô was under the influence of Bakin, and Futabatei under the influence of Sanba). We have to notice, however, that Kôyô and Rohan were the first to make intentional use of the literary essence of the Tokugawa period, which resulted in a wide revival of the interest in Saikaku. Quite paradoxically, then, the style of *Iro-zange* is more modern than that of *Ukigumo*. The style of *Iro-zange* appeared, at least to the people of those days, to be more marked by freshness than that of *Ukigumo*. This fact indicates that the evolution of style was then in progress in that direction.

The stylistic basis of Kôyô's writings is exemplified in *Iro-zange, Ni-nin Nyôbô* (Two Wives), *Kyara Makura* (Pillow of Aloes-wood Perfumery), *San-nin Zuma* (Three Wives), and *Konjiki Yasha* (A Demon of Gold). On the other hand, in an attempt to keep up with the current of the times, he wrote a number of novels in a colloquial style; among these novels, *Tonari no On-na* (The Woman in the Next-door House), *Aobudô* (Blue Grapes), *Ta-jô Ta-kon* (Tears and Regrets), and others are written in a style very similar to that of modern novels.

In their colloquial writings, Futabatei ended each sentence with *-da,* and Bimyô used *-desu;* whereas Kôyô ended each sentence with *-de-aru.* The spread of the usage of *-de-aru* is to be ascribed to Kôyô's example, and it can be said that most of the modern novels have much to owe to Kôyô as regards their style.

As for the contents of his novels, his favorite theme was the geisha quarters; and he made women the main characters in most of his novels, making much of *iki* (discreet elegance, combined with an urban polish which is an aesthetic ideal of the late Edo period). In this particular respect, his novels might be regarded as a continuation of the literature of the Edo period. His themes had much to do with the fact that his novels were regarded as realistic, in contrast with the idealistic novels by Rohan, who will be discussed shortly. Kôyô wished to express both the humor of the Edoite and the dignity of the English gentleman. This had much to do with the manner in which he tried to present an amount of reserve in his novels that would not hamper their appeal to the reading public of his time. It was because of this that the novels in his later years, such as *Ta-jô Ta-kon* and *Konjiki Yasha,* were mostly written as domestic novels. Such being the case, it seems not to have been an accident that Kôyô should have been popular with people of all ages and in all walks of life.

The views of individual and social life implied in his novels were practical. His novels do not reflect the spirit of his times, nor do they show any sign of struggle with the problems of life. They depict a practical world in which every human activity may be explained in terms of pecuniary and sexual desires, and in which stereotyped handsome men and beautiful women, good and bad, rich and poor, etc. are struggling for existence. The superficial practicality of his themes, together with the gorgeousness of his style, guaranteed the popularity of his novels with the public.

In this respect, his long masterpiece *Konjiki Yasha* is, though unfinished, certainly one of the great monuments in the literary history of the Meiji era. This novel contains a number of secular problems which can easily arouse the interest of the general public; for example, a young woman finds herself in a dilemma as to whether she should choose love, or money or social position; the young man, unrewarded in his love for the woman, attempts some kind of vengeance for her treachery by torturing himself; the unhappy domestic life among the upper class families; the heroine, confined in the exclusive circle of the upper class, cherishes the secret affection for her old lover, which evokes sympathy in the hearts of the readers. In *Konjiki Yasha*, Kôyô succeeded in integrating the elements essential for the acquisition and maintenance of ever-lasting popularity, independent of the shifting of the times. Besides, the moderate secularism in this novel seems to point out an ideal manner in which a novel may depict the affairs of human society.

Thus, Kôyô realized some of the ideals set up by *Shôsetsu Shinzui*, which had tried to 'improve novel-literature and to establish it as a legitimate branch of art capable of entertaining learned adults.' We must pay special note to Kôyô's accomplishment, because there has been no other novel that shows such a skilful integration of artistic pursuits and secularism. The peculiar traits of the naturalistic novels which came after Kôyô's have prevented the appearance of such a novel.

There were two groups of writers who participated under the leadership of Kôyô in the Kenyûsha's literary movement. One group was composed of Kôyô's friends or colleagues, such as Iwaya Sazanami, Ishibashi Shian, Hirotsu Ryûrô, Kawakami Bizan, etc. The other group consisted of his pupils, such as Izumi Kyôka, Tokuda Shûsei, Oguri Fûyô, Yanagawa Shunyô, etc. The literary activities of this group reached its climax around 1898.

Another great writer of the time who, though not a member of Kenyûsha, can be compared with Kôyô, is Kôda Rohan. Like Kôyô, he was born in Tokyo in 1867. He lived to be eighty and died in 1947. He was active as a writer for the seventeen years (1890–1906). It is noteworthy that these seventeen years coincided with the period during which Kôyô was most actively writing his novels.

It was in September of 1890 when Rohan's *Fûryû-butsu* ('A Buddhist Statue of Romance') was published, which established him as a successful novelist. It is an interesting coincidence that 1890 was the very year when Kôyô's *Iro-zange* appeared, and that *Fûryû-butsu* was published with it, as one of the series entitled *Shin-sho Hyaku-shu* (One Hundred New Novels). Like Kôyô, Rohan was under the influence of Saikaku, which can clearly be detected in his early novels. While Kôyô's novels were in all their respects stories about women; Rohan's novels, in which the main characters, representing his ideals, are depicted as remarkably heroic and masculine. Rohan's novels, thus possess a number of traits which characterize them as novels of men. The heroes of Rohan's novels are mostly professional men or men endeavoring to become masters of an art. They are described as men devoted to their fields with such enthusiasm as to be ready to sacrifice themselves for the sake of their professions. This is excellently illustrated in *Gojû no Tô* (A Five-storied Pagoda), 1892, which is one of his early masterpieces.

Such an enthusiasm and devotion to the professional arts was one of Rohan's own ideals; and his early novels exhibit his strong belief that works of art possess an ever-lasting life, independent of the artists who have created them, and surpassing even the forces of nature as well as the changing trends in the history of mankind. Rohan himself maintained this belief, though in a somewhat modified form, even into his later years. This idea of 'art for art's sake,' seasoned with the Occidental heroic air, has much in common with the culture of mind. Rohan's novels, having such themes have many elements which appealed to his reading public, at a time when stories of strenuous self-made men were widely read.

Rohan's idealism and Kôyô's realism represent the two sides of the spirit of the times. Among Rohan's novels, *Isana-tori* (A Story of a Whaler) 1892, *Hige-otoko* (A Man with a Moustache) 1897, and *Fûryû Mijin-zô* (A Treasure House of Romances), long novel serially published from 1894 to 1896, may be worth our attention. It is an interesting coincidence that Rohan's *Sora Utsu Nami* (Sky-scraping Waves, 1904 to 1906), which is regarded as marking the break of his literary activity in his early days, should have remained unfinished, just as Kôyô's last and greatest masterpiece *Konjiki Yasha* is unfinished.

Sora Utsu Nami was serially published on the Yomiuri Newspaper to take the place of *Konjiki Yasha,* which had ceased to appear there. In *Sora Utsu Nami,* Rohan deals with the problems of modern society in a very orthodox manner, something he had rarely done. He did not exhibit his own peculiar ideologies, but embodied his ideals in the form of the hero's unanswered love for his sweetheart. It is a matter for sincere regret that this novel should have remained unfinished. It is even more so, because it is quite possible that the highly refined description of the characters and the dignified formation of the plot of this novel would have opened up a new path in novel literature, had it been finished.

It seems that the pressures which caused *Sora Utsu Nami* to remain unfinished were the same as those which had such an effect upon Kôyô; i.e., the subtle changes in the current of the times. The rise of naturalism seems to have thrown Kôyô and Rohan into oblivion. However, the naturalistic novelists had to use very drastic measures to achieve their ideals; in other words, it was at the sacrifice of popularity and of the artistic flavor of their novels that they managed to achieve the purification or modernization of novel literature. Thus, the naturalists later had to witness, quite unexpectedly, a revival of the type of literature represented by *Konjiki Yasha* and *Sora Utsu Nami;* this revival manifested itself in the popular novels of the Shôwa era.

Regarding this trend in the history of modern novels, Masamune Hakuchô makes the following comment: "When I read Nakazato Kaizan's *Daibosatsu Tôge* (The Daibosatsu Pass), I felt that good old-fashioned novel writing, which had been so long suppressed by naturalism, had at last revived."

It is of course true that from a modern point of view the novels by Kôyô and Rohan seem to be possessed of a number of obviously antique traits. But they not only show us aspects of life in the past. They also demonstrate the harmonious coexistence of society and the individual, and a number of disciplines and arts which we moderns no longer possess. Thus, these novels still have something that leads us to examine our own period in the light of the spirit of the times they reflect.

It is unfortunate for us living in this modern period, as well as for Kôyô and Rohan, that their novels have not been properly recognized and appreciated as classics, but have instead fallen into oblivion.

CHAPTER VI

Ôgai, Tôkoku and Tôson

Sharing the literary scene with the Kenyûsha were such men as Mori Ôgai, Shimazaki Tôson, and Kitamura Tôkoku. Although not in the main stream of literary activity at that time, they were laying the groundwork for a new era. Tôson and Tôkoku were not novelists (at least not at the time), but their magazine, *Bungaku-kai* (Literary World) exerted a far-reaching influence on young people and nurtured a new type of literature in this country.

Shigarami Zôshi, the magazine Mori Ôgai published, was just as important a forerunner of a new type of literature.

That giant figure in Meiji Literature, Mori Ôgai's (1862–1922) most productive period was during the late Meiji and Taishô periods, but had already entered the literary scene by this time. Born in Tsuwano, Shimane Prefecture, he graduated from Tokyo Imperial University's School of Medicine in 1881 and became an army surgeon. In 1884 he went to Germany to study hygienics, returning to Japan in 1888. He went back to his job as army doctor but also set up the Shinsei Sha (New Voice Society), together with Ochiai Naobumi and others. They translated a group of European poems, *Omokage,* which appeared to *Kokumin No Tomo* (The People's Friend), and attracted a lot of attention. His novels written during this period, *Maihime* ('The Dancer'), published in *Kokumin No Tomo* in 1890, is the most important.

Maihime is colored by the author's own experiences in Germany. Toyotarô Ôta, a brilliant student, influenced by the free college life in Germany, eventually begins to question his own society which expects him to become a walking dictionary and as 'Incarnation of the Law'. It is just at this time that he meets and falls in love with a beautiful dancer, Alice. He leaves the society of his Japanese friends to live with her. They are poor but free and in love. However, finally Ôta decides he can't cut his ties with Japan and is persuaded by Baron Amagata and his friend Aizawa to give up Alice and come back to Japan and a promising future as a government official. As a result, Alice goes mad and Toyotarô feels a deep inner heart.

Because of its subject—unique to the Japanese of the day—and the powerful, tense literary style, this novel made an impression on the readers. However, the real theme of the novel apparently escaped the readers of the day, and in a sense, the author himself. It was the reverse side of the theme of Futabatei Shimei's *Ukigumo*. They both deal with the guiding principles of the way of life of the intellectuals, a new class of society in the Meiji era.

Ukigumo's Bunzô's way of thinking clashes with the realities of life and he loses his will to live, so his love is stolen by a friend and he is driven mad (or falls into a state of despondency). On the other hand, in Ôta's case, worldly ambition makes him give Alice up, although he truly loves her. While the main theme of *Ukigumo* is the unreliability of others, *Maihime* deals with mistrust of oneself. "Even my own mind is changeable", Ôta says to himself. Just like Bunzô, Ôta becomes despondent but unlike Bunzô, he is disillusioned with himself, so even worldly success will not take away his inner heart.

Both novels despict the tragic experiences of two modern young men in conflict with the feudalism of the Meiji society. But the subtle differences in character and behavior clearly reflect the different character of the writers and the different times when they were written.

Bunzô, criticized by a reader of a later day, Masamune Hakuchô, as an "Irresolute Indecisive," had no comprehension of what made the society around him tick, or at least he found it impossible to live within it. This is what led to his downfall. Toyotarô, on the other hand, is endowed with an amazing instinctive power that enables him to adjust to his surroundings. What destroys his love is not the outside society but this inner

instinct. We might say that Bunzô is more fortunate than Ôta, for although love-lorn and defeated by the society, he still believes in himself.
Ôta is a Honda with a strong conscience, a person aware of his own loneliness but who can adapt himself to reality. Despite favorable external
circumstances—fame, security, family—the darkness within his own
heart will only deepen. If we think of this in connection with the prolific
Ogai's last word, "Ridiculous", it is very interesting. There is no need to
identify the author with Toyotarô, but the mental vacuum that Toyotarô
had to face after losing the inner principles that kept him young was the
same general rate of Meiji intellectuals. It was a problem that twenty
years later Sôseki, Kafû, Futabatei, and naturalistic writers all dealt with.

Maihime is still widely read today not only because it holds a high
position among Ôgai's works as the representative book of his youth but
also because it describes a typical young man of the Meiji period.

Before writing *Maihime,* Ôgai started publishing the literary criticism
magazine *Shigarami Zôshi.* He translated and introduced foreign literary
works and wrote forceful essays on literature, drama, and art. In order to
further his efforts to introduce and plant modern artistic thought in
Japan he never refused to new intellectual arguments with people.
Yamada Bimyô, mentioned earlier, Ishibashi Ningetsu, and Toyama
Shôichi were all his opponents, but the controversy that attracted the
most attention was the so-called "No Ideal Dispute" that took place be-
tween 1891 and 1892 between him and Tsubouchi Shôyô, the editor of
Waseda Bungaku (Waseda Literature). The difference of opinion between
Shôyô and Ôgai arose a little before that when Ôgai, in his *Shigarami
Zôshi,* criticized Shôyô's articles, *Three Schools of Novelists* and *Azusa-
miko,* which appeared in the Yomiuri Newspaper, Ôgai condemned
Shôyô for compromising the stand he had taken in *Shôsetsu Shinzui* (The
Essence of the Novel) and said that he should state clearly the relative
merits of the *Three Schools.* Shôyô had contended that a critic should
not judge anything in terms of his own ideals—but take the attitude a
botanist does when studying a plant or a zoologist looking at an animal.
But Ôgai said that an ideal was a prerequisite for a critic and that when
a critic passes judgement on something, an ideal, a certain standard of

judgement is necessary. While setting forth the aesthetic theories of Hartmann, he advocated idealism.

These were the circumstances that led up to Ôgai violently attacking the phrase 'lack of ideals' that Shôyô used in his preface to *Notes and Comments of Macbeth* (in the 1st issue of *Waseda Bungaku*, Oct. 1891) and the lively debate that ensued. Shôyô said in that preface that he would refrain from criticizing and interpreting the Shakespearean masterpiece itself was without ideals, just like nature. It seems that he had Ôgai in mind when he made this comment. The dispute went on for nearly two years, lasting until June of 1892, but no conclusion was reached. All we really get when we reread it today is a clear idea of Shôyô's and Ôgai's difference in attitude toward literature and life. But it is also true that these disputes where two men, instrumental in building new literature, stated their respective views on literature helped to straighten out the literary thought of the time which was in a confused, embryonic state. Also the Young writers—the writers of the future—were influenced greatly although they may not have fully understood the contents of the dispute, the fact that literature could be a subject for serious debate made a strong impression on them.

They both had good reasons to support their contentions. What they were really argue about was how the people should be educated. Usui Yoshimi is right in saying Shôyô's opinion is based on "common sense," while calling Ôgai a "fighting, instinctive educator". In other words, Shôyô's opinion has elements that might develop into realism or naturalism, and that of Ôgai a sapling of romanticism.

Ôgai was publishing the *Shigarami Zôshi* almost singlehandedly, and often contributing to the Yomiuri Newspaper and *Kokumin No Tomo*, preparing for the coming era. He gained recognition for himself in a literary world still dominated by the Kenyûsha. Among his followers and those who worked with him on the *Shigarami Zôshi* and its successor *Mezamashi-gusa*, were new writers like Kôda Rohan, Saitô Ryokuu, Yazaki Chinshirô (Saganoya Omuro), Matsuoka (Yanagida) Kunio, Nakanishi Baika, and Takahama Kyoshi, but also many pre-Kenyûsha era writers such as Aeba Kôson and Yoda Gakkai. The mixture of old and new reflects the character of the editor Ôgai, though always absorbing the most up-to-date knowledge, never became addicted to eccentric new ideas and remained throughout his life an intelligent conservative.

There was another magazine, which started coming out a little later than the *Shigarami Zôshi,* and though it wasn't given much recognition by the literary circles of the day, took on new significance later for the turly youthful revolutionary young people who published it. It was the magazine *Bungaku-kai* (Literary World) put out by a group of young Christians led by Kitamura Tôkoku and Shimazaki Tôson.

The magazine was in existence about five years, between 1893 and 1898. Issued mainly by students of a Christian school, Meiji Gakuin, most of its members were in their twenties, such as Tôkoku and Tôson, already mentioned and Togawa Shûkotsu, Hirata Tokuboku and Baba Kochô. Also among the contributors were the young men who would later represent a new age such as Ueda Bin, Matsuoka Kunio, Higuchi Ichiyô and Kunikida Doppo. They were influenced by Christianity which was the object of both belief and scepticism of the intellectuals and also represented a progressive side of phase culture of the day and also Western European literature—mostly English and American—which was imported along with Christianity. Using Christianity and Western European literature as a base, they tried to write fresh new literature completely disassociated from the literary traditions of the end of the Edo period. The romanticism movement of the Bungaku-kai played a pioneering role in modernizing our literature.

Bungaku-kai had something in common with *Mezamashi-gusa* in that it was issued by writers who were not content with the "Western-dressed literature" of the Kenyûsha and were seeking more advanced literary thoughts and works. There was a difference, however, in that many of the contributors to the *Mezamashi-gusa* were scholars and established writers who were prone to think of literature as a cultural side interest while the young unknowns of the *Bungaku-kai* instinctively felt that literature could take the place of religion in the inner lives of modern men and devoted themselves to this mission. It was their zeal that enabled them to launch a truly meaningful literary movement, and though their works were immature and often caused friction between the existing trends of the times, they had a big influence on future young generations. It has become evident over the years that the first pure flame of romanticism in this country—though faint and dull—*Bungaku-kai* was an important gate way to, and corner stone of, modern Japanese literature.

Kitamura Tôkoku, who took his own life while still in his youth, and Shimazaki Tôson, who made an unending effort to spread Tôkoku's influence on the world and who left a big mark on literary history, first as a poet and later as a novelist, symbolize the two sides of the movement.

Kitamura Tôkoku (real name: Montarô) was born in Odawara, Kanagawa Prefecture, in the first year of Meiji, 1868. He came up to Tokyo in 1881 and studied at the Tokyo Semmon Gakkô (which later became Waseda University). While in college, he was influenced by the democratic right movement and for a while took part in political movements. In 1889 he published Soshû No Shi (The Prisoner's Poem) and in 1891, Hôraikyoku (The Song of Mt. Horai)—unique long dramatic poems. From around 1894, he began publishing many essays including critiques of the traditional novels of Kôyô and Rohan. As the very titles of his essays such as "The Secret Palace in the Human Heart," "On a Virgin's Chastity," and "Pondering on the Muse of Mt. Fuji," suggest Tôkoku had a unique poetical style with which he discussed various problems of life from a fresh romantic standpoint. The fact that he never reached maturity that would have enabled him to gain more influence over his contemporaries, actually guaranteed him a more lasting place on literary history.

After the first issue of *Bungaku-kai* came out, he opposed Yamaji Aizan's utilitarianism saying that the value of literature was something other than utilitarianism. He wrote many forceful essays on literature, religion and philosophy in *Jogaku-Zasshi, Heiwa,* and *Kokumin No Tomo.* But on his personal life he felt more and more stifled and in 1894 took his personal life.

Shimazaki Tôson while deeply influenced by Tôkoku led a very different life from him.

He was born in Magome in Nagano prefecture in 1872 and happened to come to Tokyo the same year Tôkoku did 1881. He entered Meiji Gakuin in 1887 and was baptised the next year. He graduated in 1891. He did translations which appeared in *Jogaku-Zasshi* (Women 'students' Magazine) and elsewhere. In 1893 he was in charge of the first issue of *Bungaku-kai*. Under the pen name Kotôan he published *"Hikyoku Biwa-hôshi"* and poems that were later included in *"Wakanashû"* (Young Herbs: An Anthology of Poems).

In the meantime Tôson left the Christian faith, resigned as professor of Meiji Womens School and started a wondering trip. He started teaching at Tôhoku Gakuin in Sendai and in 1897 published *Wakanashû* and the next year *"Hitohabune"* ('One Leaf Vessel: A Collection'). Finally in 1899 he became a professor at Komoro Gijuku, where he stayed for six full years.

During that time he was meditating and writing, laying the foundation for his later writing. He wrote descriptions of nature along the line of Ruskin. The foreign novels of such writers as Flaubert, Goncourt, Hauptmann, Dostoevski, made him see life and art in a new light.

His short stories such as *"Kyûshujin"* (Former Master), *"Warazôri"* (Straw Sandals), *"Oyaji"* (An Old Man), *"Rôjô"* (An Old Maid), *"Suisai Gaka"* (The Water Color Painter), *"Yashi-no-Hagakure"* (Under the Leaves of Palm), *"Tsugaru-Kaikyô"* (Tsugaru Strait), showed the influence of these foreign writers but were also preparation for his shift from the lyric poet who wrote *"Wakanashû"* to the central novelist in the naturalism movement.

CHAPTER VII

Kôson, Ryokuu and Ichiyô

Now let's take a look at another group of minor writers—also contemporary with the Kenyûsha—who give an impression of being behind the times for their close connection with the literature of a former age. However, through their superior individuality, they left a legacy far greater than that of the commonplace writers of the day who were up with the times.

The senior member of the group is Aeba Kôson, a member of the Negishi group and the last living survivor of the Edo Gesaku tradition. Born in 1855 in the Shitaya district of Edo, he studied from an early age Gesaku under Takabatake Ransen. He was employed by the Yomiuri Shimbun in 1873; his stories appeared in serial form in that paper. By the time *Shôsetsu Shinzui* and *Ukigumo* came out, he was already the dean of the traditional literature school. Well-versed in Edo period literature and showing a particular propensity for Hachimonjiya books, he developed a style close to that of Ukiyo Zôshi. In this respect he was a forerunner of the Kôyô-Rohan Genroku literature revival. His works of the early part of Meiji—later compiled into an anthology, *Muratake* (Cluster of Bamboo)—stood out above all the imitations of Gesaku works published in Bunka-Bunsei era. The revival of Genroku literature (connected with the rise of nationalism) had an adverse effect on Shôyô and Futabatei's reputation but made people see Kôson's real value. In 1889 Kôson's *Horidashimono* (Lucky Find) came out in *Shincho-Hyakushû* (Collection of New Works) along with Kôyô's *Irozange* (Amourous Confessions) and Rohan's *Furyûbutsu* (A Buddhist Statue of Romance) and was highly praised by Ôgai. The same year, his *Tôsei Shônin Kishitsu* (Character of Modern Merchants) was published. The next year his *Kachidoki* (Shout of Victory) was included in Shunyô-Dô's *Shinsaku Jûniban* (Twelve New Stories.) He was active in the literary world until close to 1907, and highly esteemed as a writer outside of the Kenyûsha tradition. His favourite authors extended from Ejimaya Kiseki and Ryûtei Tanehiko to Saikaku and Chikamatsu and, in his later years, Bakin. He did a special study on Bakin.

Kôson's works are characterized by their light and simple style. We do not get the heavy, oppressive feeling we see in Kôyô's artificial, ornamental early works. We can attribute this less to a difference in models, for they both imitated Edo writers, than Kôson's more thorough knowledge of Gesaku literature.

Kôson's style is, literally speaking, not colloquial, but it is very close to the spirit of colloquial writing. The reason Futabatei "imitated Samba, Mr. Kôson, and Hachimonjiya books" in chapter one of *Ukigumo* is that he found in those works ideal examples of "the colloquial spirit."

Kôson's novels were well received for the vivid, flowing style and the writer's affable, witty personality. But actually they had nothing to do with the new age. Though he excelled in describing segments of the society still overshadowed by the preceeding period, his characters and his observations and criticism of them were stereotyped, based on the conventional Giri-Ninjô (love and duty) For this reason he was completely cut off the literary currents of the age after 1907.

Right up until his death in 1922, however, he continued writing drama criticism under the name of Takenoya-Shujin, which he had begun in 1889 when he entered Asahi Shimbun. He started a new trend in Kabuki criticism and was recognized as one of the foremost authorities in that field.

In short, Kôson was the last man who really lived in the cultural tradition of the Edo period. With his self-righteousness—that came out in his moderate narrow-mindedness, characteristic of traditional merchant families, and his unselfishness—he, and his works, too, were doomed to lose out in the new Meiji civilization.

As the fact that he had a free flowing style—unusual for a writer in his day—suggests, he could easily keep the cultural self-respect that so many other writers over-anxious to absorb Western culture lost. This characteristic was especially evident in his travel essays and criticism.

If Kôson was like a declining merchant, Saitô Ryokuu, the son of the family doctor of the Tôdôs, a feudal clan, could be compared to a degenerate low-class Samurai. Ryokuu was born in 1867 in Kobe and taken to Tokyo by his father when he was 10 years old. Living in Midori-cho, Honjo, he quickly became familiar with the 'downtown' atmosphere of Tokyo. He learned Haikai from Kikakudô Eiki, studied under Kanagaki Robun and contributed Gesaku-style short stories to Eiri Shimbun (Illustrated Newspaper) under the pen name Kôtô Midori. Around 1889 he began writing criticism under the name of Shôjiki Shôdayu and established a place for himself for the sharp criticism and light parody in *Shôsetsu Hasshû* (Eight Basics of the Novel) in 1889, *Shogaku Shôsetsu Kokoroe* (Beginners' Instruction on the Novel) in 1890, *Bungaku Hitokarage* (Literature Summed Up) in 1893, and *Shintai-Shi Mihon* (A Sample of New Style Poetry) in 1894. The two novels, *Abura-Jigoku* (Hell of Oil), that came out in January 1891, and *Kakurenbo* (Hide-and-Seek), published in July of the same year, won him a reputation as a novelist. They both dealt with Yanagibashi, one of Tokyo's gay quarters. *Abura-Jigoku* was particularly well received for its frank and ironic treatment of a naive boy's unrequitted love for a Geisha. But Ryokuu himself preferred *Kakurembo,* which depicted the "skill" of a rich playboy. Tsubouchi Shôyô also cited *Kakurembo* as Ryokuu's representative work, praising its "conciseness."

Next Ryokuu wrote novels like *Kadojamisen* (Shamisen Player at the Gate), which appeared in 1895, but his refined tastes and highly polished style ran counter to the times. Because of his limited scope and lack of originality in observation of human life, all his stories were variations of the same theme. In addition, the fact that he could not rid himself of the flavour of Bunka-Bunsei literature explain his short-lived life as a novelist and the limited number of his works.

However, he was fortunate enough to have more intrinsic talent as a critic.

Uchida Roan once said that though Ryokuu had his roots in the Gesaku tradition he showed instinctive interests in the new literary trend and had constant and close association with young new-intellectuals, the followers of his own teacher, Kanagaki Robun, Shôyô, Rohan, Ôgai, Mannen, Seisetsu, Reiun, Ichiyô and Kochô. Roan said that though Ryokuu had no formal education, he was always an intelligent sympathizer of the new literary trend. We should not forget that behind his cynical pose he had an outstanding sense as a journalist.

This talent explains his constant association with numerous newspapers, such as Konnichi Shimpô (Today's Journal), Kokkai (National Diet), Kôko Shimbun, Niroku Shimbun and Yorozuchôhô.

He had long been a close friend of Ôgai's and was a regular contributor to Shigarami-zôshi. In the spring of 1896, Ôgai and Rohan began putting out joint, anonymous reviews of novels, Sannin Jôgo (Three Men's Redundancies) and in the autumn of the same year Yoda Gakkai, Morita Shiken, Kôyô and Kôson joined the three in writing Unchû-Go (Words in the Clouds) which continued coming out until September, 1898. As Tayama Katai later recalled, the reviews were both dreaded by and yet enlightening to many writers of the day for their wide knowledge and to-the-point irony based on their sharp insight.

His aphoristic essays, in Oboe-chô (Memorandum, 1901), Hikae-chô (Notebook, 1898), and Ganzen Kôwa (Private Talks, 1898) are the most unique of his works and still read and appreciated by some people for their wit, irony and satire—qualities rare in Meiji literature. In his old age, he was in poor health, impoverished and had lost contact with many of his friends. He died in misery in 1904. Shortly before his death, he wrote the following obituary for himself: "I hereby announce my happy death on this day, April 1. Ryokuu Saitô." His friends put it in newspapers after his death.

"Alas, the man who once lived in the joys and passions of the gay quarters of Edo, was at last unable to struggle for existence any longer in the 20th century society,"—the 26-year-old Nagai Kafû, in the United States at the time, wrote in his diary.

Saitô Ryokuu died at 38, an early death compared to Aeba Kôson who lived to be 68, but Higuchi Ichiyô died still younger, when she was only 24 years old.

She was born in the spring of 1872 and died in the autumn of 1896, enjoying a reputation as a first-rate novelist during a lifetime of only 24 years and some odd months. There are few parallels in the history of Japanese literature, or for that matter, in that of other countries either.

Ichiyô's father was the son of a farmer in Yamanashi Prefecture. During the Ansei period (1854–1859) he came up to Edo and after the Meiji Restoration worked at the Tokyo Prefectural Office and the Police Department. In 1887, he retired and failing in an business enterprise with some friends died soon.

Before this, his eldest son had died, his second son married and moved away, and his eldest daughter been disowned for marrying someone the family did not approve of. Therefore, after her father's death, Ichiyô became the head of the impoverished household and had the responsibility of providing for her mother and younger sister.

While her father was still living, Ichiyô had begun studying *waka* poem in the Haginoya school of Nakajima Utako and became known as one of the 'Big Three' poetesses of Haginoya (along with Tanabe Tatsuko —later Miyake Kahô—and Itô Natsuko.) After her father's death, however, the family was so hard up that in 1889, the year after he died, Ichiyô had to earn money as a manual labourer with her mother and sister.

It is said that Ichiyô was first inspired to write a novel after her friend Tanabe Tatsuko made her name known in 1888 with her novel *Yabu no Uguisu* (A Nightingale in a Bush) taken after Shôyô's *Tôsei Shosei Katagi*. A chance visit in 1891 to Nakarai Tôsui, a novelist writing for the Asahi Shimbun, set her on the path to becoming a writer. Tôsui, a popular writer who mainly wrote serial stories for the newspaper, made some rewriting on a work Ichiyô had written, and published it in his magazine, *Musashino*. It seems there was a rapport close to love between Ichiyô and Tôsui, who had just lost his wife. Next through Tanabe Tatsuko, Ichiyô had *Umoregi* (The Fossil Wood) and *Akezukiyo* (Morning Moon) published in the magazine, *Miyako no Hana;* the next year, 1892, through Hirata Tokuboku she had *Yukinohi* (A Snowy Day) and other novels published in *Bungakukai.* Her family moved to Ryûsenji, Shitaya, the scene of her later masterpiece, *Takekurabe* (Comparing Heights). In *Ôtsugomori* (The Last Day of the Year), which came out in Bungaku-kai in late 1894, she showed remarkable improvement in her style.

There was nothing new or different about her early works—the sentences seemed old-fashioned even in her own day, the adverse effect of her *waka* background, and she used too many vulgar techniques, possibly Tôsui's influence. Even *Umoregi,* which is said to have been written when she was on bad terms with Tôsui, was a poor imitation of Rohan.

But the life of poverty she led during this immature, developmental period, her resistances to it and a deepened knowledge of the world and the human mind, awakened the intrinsic poetic spirit that lay deep within her, which, possibly enhanced by her ill health, blossomed out into an unparalleled flower of youthful literature during a brief period after her first truly original work, *Ôtsugomori.* Still not very well known, Ichiyô began to write *Takekurabe* for Bungaku-kai early in 1895, the year before her death. In May of the same year, with the appearance of her *Yuku Kumo* (Passing Cloud) in *Taiyô* and in September of one of her representative works, *Nigorie* (Muddy Stream) in Bungei Club, she attracted the attention of the world and was recognized as an up-and-coming writer along with Kawakami Bizan and Izumi Kyôka.

Probably because of her declining health, she did not write much in 1896, the year she died, but a republication of *Ôtsugomori* in Taiyô in February and a complete *Takekurabe* (thus far published in segments) in Bungei Club in April, won her the highest praise from the leading literary men of the age like Ôgai, Rohan, Ryokuu and Chogyû. One of the Unchû-go reviewers mentioned earlier placed *Takekurabe* above "Zola and Ibsen", saying "I may be laughed at by the world for being an Ichiyô worshipper, but I would not hesitate to call her a true poet".

She died in the autumn of that year, but her reputation, in a sense, is still going up today.

Tayama Katai said that the lavish praise on Ichiyô is partly attributable to the antipathy of big literary men like Ôgai and Rohan against other more progressive young writers. This may be true to some extent.

It was also true that good reputation given to her partly resulted from sympathy for a girl who built up her abilities in the midst of poverty and died on the threshold of fame.

However, the fact remains that anyone who reads Ichiyô's works today cannot help but feel behind her old-fashioned style the unusual passion of a burning soul, that is not found in Kôyô, Rohan, even in Ôgai.

Ichiyô's originality lies in her means of expression. She borrowed Saikaku's sentence style and without changing it brought it to life by using it to describe the deepest of her own experiences. She made a better use of the pseudo-classic sentence style, a product of that age, than any of her contemporaries.

Of course it would be absurd to expect wide-range observations on life and society from an unmarried women of 24. Iwaki Juntarô has justly stated that "Miss Ichiyô's novels do not describe various aspects of life in order to depict nature, but portray only specific aspects of life in order to express her own view on life."

As he says, her novels show a tendency "to be based on one view of life and describe only one character." And "There is no attempt to vary the plot. All her works are nothing but a set of examples to illustrate the same thing." But this "theme" was the one she devoted her life to, and the "one character" that kept appearing was throbbing with the sympathy of the author.

Like any young person who dies without fulfilling his ambition, she dealt with the theme of the struggle between young individuality trying to grow and the pressures of the society on it. It was a theme that was to develop into what is called the "serious novel" or "ideological novel", but the true poetic sympathy that flows between her characters and herself gives her works a value other writers failed to have. At the same time, however, to say that all her works describe an adult world as viewed by a child is a justified criticism. This limit of hers is suggested by the fact that her best work is *Takekurabe,* a story dealing with the world of children. Nonetheless, no novel equals *Takekurabe,* in its poetic and yet accurate description of the subtle feelings of boys and girls in the transition from childhood to adulthood. No author can express all aspects of life, and an author who has vividly caught just one segment of life—even if in only one work—is, therefore, immortal. This principle is particularly true in the case of a talented author who dies young.

As is often true with the case of a writer who dies young, as time goes by growing interests have been shown not only in her works but also in the personality of the author behind the works. As a result, Ichiyô's diary has come to be prized as much as her novels. In a sense Ichiyô and Tôkoku (who died two years before her), were twins. With the acknowledgement of the value of their works, they became increasingly attractive to later generations for the possibilities glimpsed at but never fully developed in their works.

These two unyielding souls, who were defeated in their respective struggles for living, and died one before and one after the Sino-Japanese War, were symbolic of the mal-treatment Meiji society gave its writers. At the same time they were the twin stars which will for ever continue to shine in memory of the modern Japanese literature at its youthful stage.

CHAPTER VIII

From Ideological Novel to Social Novel

The ten-year period between 1895 and 1905, or between the end of the Sino-Japanese War and the end of the Russo-Japanese War, was of special significance in the history of the modern Japanese novel. In contrast to the last decade of the Meiji period, the age of naturalism, it is usually referred to as the golden age of romantic literature. The representative types of literature were poetry and criticism; novels falling back to the second place. Tôson's *Wakanashû* and other anthologies of poetry, Yosano Tekkan's magazine, *Myôjô* (first issue, April 1900), Tsuchii Bansui's *Tenchi Ujô* (Heaven and Earth Have Feelings), Susukida Kyûkin's *Botekishû* (Evening Flute, 1899) and Kambara Ariake's *Dokugen Aika* (1903) were all products of this period. Yosano Akiko's *Midaregami* (Tangled Hair, 1901) perfectly represents this romantic tide.

It was also during this period that Shiki, following his Haiku activities, revolutionized Tanka, and Takayama Chogyu's lyric-like essays moved many young people as they had never been before.

As was true of romantic literature in many countries, the novel of the day, as an expression of the spirit of the times, stepped aside for poetry and criticism. And yet, considered from the point of view of the history of the development of the novel, this was an interesting transitional period when the novel showed various budding potentialities.

The main currents were: the ideological and serious novels of the younger Kenyûsha men like Kawakami Bizan, Hirotsu Ryûrô, Izumi Kyôka, Oguri Fûyô; Zolaism represented by Kosugi Tengai, Nagai Kafû in early days, and sometimes by Fûyô and the social novels starting with

Tokutomi Roka and Uchida Roan and extending to Kinoshita Naoe.

These novelists are usually looked down on by literary historians as a 'valley' between the two 'peaks'—Kenyûsha literature and Naturalism—or as the 'tail-end' of the formative second decade of the Meiji period. Admittedly there were not many great novelists among them, and those of them who did have exceptionally long careers as novelists, like Kyôka or Kafû, had such a different style in their later works that hardly a trace of this period remained.

Of course, it is true that the novels of this period had many features that justified the later criticism by naturalists who labeled them "obsolete", and that few of them had the pure artistic quality of the early works of Ôgai, Kôyô and Rohan. But if we look at all of Meiji era as one large transitional period in literature, we can describe this period as a transition within a transition. Many problems that people of the preceding era had not thought of developed out of this period and buds, that were later nipped off in the artistic sophistication, tried to bloom.

By this time Japan was beginning to have the semblance of a modern nation in all areas of her culture, and people also came to be aware of some of the dangers of modernization. Japan revised in her favour treaties with Western nations as a result of her victory in the Sino-Japanese War. There was a rapid industrial growth, particularly in the realm of light industry and the gold standard was adopted in Japan. However, being forced by Russia, France and Germany for the return of the Liaotung Peninsula to China and then menace of Russia from the north gave rise to nationalistic feeling and a military buildup. The national unity during the Sino-Japanese War ameliorated the conflicts between the regional clans and the Liberal Party. As the National Diet gradually turned to a place of political compromise and bargaining, young people's outcry for freedom and ideals of liberation, which had until then only been expressed as political fervor, began seeking an outlet in religion and literature and penetrating deeper into their daily lives. Their ideals collided with feudalistic customs which still entrenched every corner of the society, but at the same time awakened a sense of individuality in them and prodded them to fight for justice and freedom.

Behind the romantic literature of this period was this wide-spread upsurge of humanism in Japan. Shimazaki Tôson, recalling this period later said:

"At last the time of the new poetry has come. It was like a beautiful dawn. Some cried out like ancient prophets, and some sang out like Occidental poets. Everyone seemed to be as though intoxicated by a brilliant light, a new voice and fanciful thoughts."

One of the characteristics of this movement was that the literary zeal was not, like ten years before, a thing limited to the elite; it found sympathizers and followers all over the country. The following incident typifies the period: Ôtori Akiko, a Sakai girl, came to Tokyo, married Yosano Tekkan, editor of *Myôjô* and became a famous poetess.

With such a background, the novel took a new turn than it did in the preceding decade.

The new trend began to appear around 1895. In 1895 Kawakami Bizan wrote *Ôsakazuki* (Large Cup), *Shokikan* (Secretary) and *Uraomote* (Both Sides of a Thing), Ryûro published *Hemeden* (Ugly-Eyed Denkichi) and *Kurotokage* (Black Lizard) and Kyôka, *Yakô Junsa* (Police on Night Patrol) and *Gekashitsu* (Surgical Room). Novels by some of the new writers including *Arinosusabi* (Let it be there) by Gotô Chûgai and *Nyôbo-goroshi* (Killing Your Wife) by Emi Suiin, also indicated this literary trend. In 1896, famous works like Ryûro's *Imado Shinjû* (Double Suicides at Imado) and Kyôka's *Teriha Kyôgen* (Teriha Play) and *Ichinomaki* (The First Volume), in addition to Fûyô's *Neoshiroi* (Powdering at Night) and Chûgai's *Yami no Utsutsu* (Sobre mind in the Dark) were published. Of these writers, Kyôka and Bizan were the first to write clearly-defined ideological novels. Kyôka's *Yakô Junsa* and *Gekashitsu,* and Bizan's *Shokikan* and *Uraomote,* were said to be representative of this kind of novels. The term idealistic novel was used in contrast to the "realistic novel" of Kôyô in the preceding period. Iwaki Juntarô explained that an idealistic novel is not one that describes things realistically, but that it is "built on a certain concept or leaning from which the characters' and their psychological development derived," and that the writer of this kind of novel tries to capture "something other than mere realistic description."

To take an example, *Yakô Junsa* (1895), which established Izumi Kyô-ka's reputation as a novelist, tells the story of a policeman faithful to his duty who gave his life to save the father of the girl he loved although he was trying to keep them apart. 'Duty' wins out over 'personal feelings of love' in this story. By having a common man embody his own highest ideals Kyôka opened up a whole new world not found in Kôyô or Rohan, but in a sense, a combination of the two. Kyôka drew with this and his next work, *Gekashitsu*, the attention of the literary world as a new hope in the modern Japanese literature.

But Kyôka's style did not develop into the social novel, the direction suggested by *Yakô Junsa* and *Gekashitsu*. The series of works, beginning with *Ichinomaki* and ending with *Chikainomaki* (Volume of Oath), published the following year, and *Teriha Kyôgen*, were already along the lines of sweet romantic novels, childhood recollections flavored with a sort of feminism. These characteristics were even more evident in his following works, *Tatsumi Kôdan* (Episode in Town, 1898) and *Tsuya Monogatari* (Tale of Vigils, 1898). He was a born romanticist, rare in the history of the modern Japanese novel. Rather than describing things as they were—he created unique characters out of his own ethical and aesthetic beliefs and was intoxicated by the world he created. In both *Kôya Hijiri* (Travelling Monk, 1900) and *Fûryûsen* (Railway Line of Romance, 1903), although very different, Kyôka displayed a highly developed skill for writing strange stories. Even with the rise of Naturalism around 1907, he stuck to his own style and even improved on it in such masterpieces as *Onna-keizu* (Lineage of Women, 1907), *Shirasagi* (Snowy Heron, 1909). After that, although he isolated himself from the local literary world, he was respected by a group of writers like Satomi Ton, Akutagawa Ryûnosuke, Minakami Takitarô and Kubota Mantarô and many readers and kept writing until his death in 1939.

His literature was, as Minakami Takitarô put it, a literature of "resistance and yearning", and the sense of social justice, seen in his early works, was alive to the end in the form of the will power or courage of the heroines even though it became burried in a strange world of beauty. This resistance against power, however, did develop into a social novel that depicts contemporary (society) on a wider scale, partly because of his aesthetics summed up by Minakami as follows. "His primary aim was to give an impression of truth not by describing things just as they are, but by describing impossibilities."

The immaturity of the modern society around him and his own arti-san-like admiration for the feudalistic idea of Giri-ninjô (love and duty) should also be taken into account. Anyway, he was a writer who had a poetic imagination rarely found in a modern Japanese novelist. His vigorous and long-lived creative power and the strong passion expressed by characters in his novels made him mutant of the Kenyûsha and also give us an impression of something different from the traditional light-coloured Japanese literature. In this respect, it is interesting that Okuno Shintarô has recently pointed out the possible influence of Chinese liter-ature on Kyôka through popular novels of the Edo period.

While Izumi Kyoka was in various respects a fortunate novelist, Kawa-kami Bizan was an unfortunate one. Born in 1869 in Osaka, he came to Tokyo with his family. He became acquainted with Kôyô and Bimyô while he was preparing to enter Tokyo University, and took part in the establishment of Kenyûsha. But it was not until 1895, that with the pub-lication of Ôsakazuki and Uraomote mentioned earlier, he finally made a name for himself as a novelist. These works with their "serious way of thinking and observing things" were regarded as representative of a new trend of the times.

Also known as an excellent composer of Haiku and Haibun (poetical essay with a tone of a Haiku), Bizan was known as the Yokoi Yayû (renowned poet of Genroku period) of the day. In Futokoro Nikki (Pocket Diary), a travel journal of a trip to Miura Peninsula, published in 1901 this feeling for poetry came out most clearly. However, because of family circumstances and a highly nervous temperament, he had been so haunted by illusions and sleep-walking from early in his life, that he lived in an entirely different world from healthy men of common sense like Kôyô and Rohan. His ideological novels, too, can be regarded as reflections on his abnormally sensitive nerves of social evils, which finally came to people's attention after the Sino-Japanese War. *Shokikan* described a link between bureaucrats and a political merchant, and implied that the merchant's daughter would have to be sacrificed for her father's benefit. *Uraomote* is the story of a man known for his charitable works in the day time, but is a thief by night, and who commits suicide at the end to transcend good and evil. A dismal pessimism, rather than a satirical tone, runs through his works.

Considering the combination of this peculiar philosophy and his well-constructed plots and sentences, it was only natural that his novels gathered a reputation. Today, however, these early works are hardly readable since the characters seem stereotyped. Iwaki Juntarô has justly said that Bizan was "so intent on expressing his ideals that the happenings seem far from natural. He was so earnest in expressing his social viewpoint that the psychological changes were not described clearly. It is regretable that these works fall short of being outstanding works of art".

In his later years, however, he matured as a writer. In *Kannon Iwa* (The Rock of the Goddess of Mercy), which started appearing in the Kokumin Shimbun in 1905 and was completed and published as a book in 1907. In his short stories, such as *Yûdasuki* (Cotton Tasuki), he began to show superb style and writing skill. He committed suicide on June 15, 1908. Some say he was tired of struggling with poverty while others believe that he was distressed artistically.

Tayama Katai attributed Bizan's suicide to the agony of being left behind by the rising currents of naturalism, while Futabatei, who heard the sad news during his voyage to Russia, wrote to his wife: "I was surprised at Bizan's suicide. How awful the life of a writer is!."

Hirotsu Ryûrô's style was similar to Bizan, and in a sense, his fate was too. Ryûrô was born in Nagasaki in 1861. At first he wanted to be a physician, but he became civil servant for several years after 1881, but started his writing career with the appearance of a serial novel Joshi Sanseiken Shinkirô (The Mirage of Woman Suffrage) in the Tokyo Eiri (Illustrated) Shimbun in 1887. He was counted among the representative new writers after *Hemeden* (Ugly-eyed Denkichi) and *Kurotokage* (Black

Lizard) came out in 1895. He came to be regarded as a great writer of the new age with famous works like *Kawachiya* and *Imado Shinjû* (Double Suicide at Imado) that came out in 1896. Though his works were commonly known as tragic novels basically, they were no different from Bizan's idealogical novels. They were given a different name because despite the same propensity for tragic subjects, Ryûrô had more skill than Bizan in describing things realistically. *Imado Shinjû* tells the story of Yoshizato, a prostitute of the Yoshiwara gay quarter, who was forced to part from a patron she loved, Hirata; but when she learned that another patron Zenkichi, whom she had been treating coolly, had gone bankrupt because of her, gave him all her money and eventually committed suicide with him out of pity and despair. Mixed in with the story is a description of Yoshiwara in winter. Yoshizato's unconscious vacillations of mind between Hirata and Zenkichi are concisely depicted.

But after the publication of *Chikushô-bara* (The Twins) in 1897, Ryuro began turning out too many works, few of them really good. After writing short works like *Yawata no Kyôjo* (The Mad Woman of Yawata) in 1901, *Ame* (The Rain) in 1902, the drama *Meguro Kôdan* (The Episode at Meguro) in 1905 and the novel *Kokoro no Hi* (The Flame of the Mind) in 1908, he began to isolate himself from the literary world, publishing few works, and died in 1928.

"My father had no connection with the literary world in his late years. He was sad and lonesome,"—writes Hirotsu Kazuo, the second son of Ryûrô. Ryûrô, in his late years said to Kazuo: "The reason I could not write any more was because I began to reflect on myself. A writer can develop more by going straight on, keeping his eyes straight forward, not looking back."

He is also quoted as saying:

"A man should be self-conceited and arrogant. I lacked both qualities."

This remark is not simply the self-depreciation of Ryûrô alone, but the common lament of all his contemporary writers with a cosmopolitan upbringing and education. No one would be surprised to hear the same thing coming from by Ryokuu, Bizan, or Futabatei.

The remark has something which suggests the situation of the literary

man of all ages. If as Kunikida Doppo pointed out the naturalistic movement was the biggest turning point in modern Japanese literature, then
we could also say that these writers, because they were the losers at this
turning point of history, grasped an aspect of truth in literature, but at a
cost too high to pay.

While Bizan and Ryûrô were almost contemporaries of Kôyô and
other members of Kenyûsha, there were some other men who made
their debut a little later, which gave them a better chance of developing
themselves in the new age. Among them were Fûyô, Tengai and Kafû.
There was a difference in their ages: Tengai, the eldest, was born in 1865,
Fûyô in 1875 and Kafû, 1879. But they all started their literary careers as
followers of Ryokuu, Kôyô and Ryûrô, and by inheriting one aspect or
the other of their styles.

In the beginning Kosugi Tengai studied under Saitô Ryokuu and first
appeared in the literary world as a satirist, writing works like *Kibyô* (The
Strange Malady, 1895), *Kairyô Wakatono* (The Young Gentleman Re-
formist) and *Sotoba-ki* (The Record of Grave) both in 1896. But it was
under the influence of the French naturalist writer Emile Zola that he
really developed his own individuality. First, he declared that the "way
artistic beauty affects a human being should be like the way a natural
phenomenon touches on the human senses"—Preface to *Hatsu-sugata*
(The Young Figure, 1900). And then, he developed this concept further:
"Nature is Nature. It is neither good, evil, beautiful or ugly. It is just that
someone in a certain country in a certain age, takes a segment of Nature,
and arbitrarily labels it good, bad, beautiful or ugly. The novel is the
nature of the world of thought. Nobody has the right to say what should
be written and what should not about anything good, evil, beautiful, or
ugly"—Preface to *Hayari Uta* (Popular Song) in 1902.

The two prefaces above are famous as the first concrete examples of the
influence of French naturalism on a Japanese writer, but the words themselves probably have far more meaning then Tengai was aware of. Considering the large part naturalism played later in the history of the Japanese novel, they are worth examining.

The first thing explained here is that nature exists independent of human value judgements based on beauty, ugliness, good, or evil. Of course this way of thinking is backed up by the developments in natural science, and forms the universal basis of modern man's feelings toward life, though there are various individual differences. Needless to say this way of thinking was upheld by French naturalist writers, many of whom were atheists and determinists. This kind of a dual thought can be traced back to Descartes. French romanticists, too, used to sing of the disparity between nature and human beings.

It is interesting that before he was influenced by Zola who advocated naturalism, Tengai took the fundamentals and basics of his overall modern thought. But we should not criticize Tengai for not fully understanding Zolaism—he took from him only what he needed.

As I mentioned earlier, Shôyô's ultimate purpose in writing *Shôsetsu Shinzui* was to free literature from ethical utilitarianism. Tengai tried to complete this liberation process with the help of 'science', liberating nature (or Man as a part of nature) from all standards of beauty, ugliness, good and evil—in other words, standards of ethics and aesthetics. For, according to him, beauty and ugliness, good and evil are relative, arbitrary things which differ from age to age and nation to nation. Therefore, describing the realities of human life—which had become accepted as the established aim of the novel after *Shôsetsu Shinzui*—meant freeing it from all relative norms and letting it return to nature.

The same way of thinking is expressed by Nagai Kafû in the postscript to his *Jigoku no Hana* (Flower in Hell), published in 1902, when he was twenty-four. "Man has an animal-like side in his personality."

This remark indicates that the idea of liberating man from the established moral and aesthetic standards by looking at him as a part of Nature or an animal was not Tengai's own idea, but the general trend of the times that he expounded in Zola's name.

The strange statement, "The novel is the nature of the world of thought," can only be understood in this context. What Tengai wanted to say was that the novel must aim at the truth, like 'Nature,' free from the human society's standards of good and evil, beauty and ugliness. As you can imagine this is exactly what Zola asserted.

Unlike Zola, however, Tengai failed to realize that nature conceived in this way is based on scientific knowledge, and that literature based on nature must set up its own scientific method. Anyway, Tengai could not put the idea into practise in his works. While Zola, following the theories of Claud Bernard and Prospierre Lucas, replaced personality with temperament as the principal element in the novel and painted an enormous fresco of the society, Tengai only superficially imitated the Les Rougon-Macquart books. The concept of 'heredity and environment,' the backbone of Zola's works, was no more than a figure of speech to him.

Needless to say, in the experimental novel, advocated by Zola and based on medical determinism, the experiments in natural science, which are inquiries into Nature, were equated with the process of constructing literary works within the minds of novelists. It should be regarded as the appearance of the scientific illusions of Zola's age in literature, rather than an application of the scientific spirit to literature. However, Zola could fabricate this way of thought into a system, and make it live within the inner framework of his novels.

Tengai, however, took in Zolaism in its extended (or retrogressive) form, as an overall scheme of modern thought, or on the surface, merely as a new technique or design. It was not only Tengai. Fûyô, as well as Kafû and Tôson of that period, and other new writers of the day who turned their eyes toward Western literature, all took in Western writers in this way. This is why their literature was a reflection of the spirit of the times, and nothing more.

The years 1901 and 1902 formed an interesting period in this respect. *Hatsusugata* and *Hayariuta* by Tengai, *Jigoku no Hana* by Kafû and *Sametaru Onna* by Fûyô are some examples.

It was a period when the sense of individuality and liberation that were brewed in the midst of the romantic tide began to take a definite form in literary works. Among the works published in 1901 were Yosano Akiko's *Midaregami* (mentioned earlier), Toson's *Rakubai-Shû* (Fallen Plums: A Collection of Poems), Roka's *Omoide no Ki* (Recollections), and Takayama Chogyu's essays, *"Literary Men as Culural Critics,"* and *"On the Aesthetic Life."* In 1902 Ôgai's *Sokkyô Shijin,* actually a translation of

Andersen's *Improvisatoren* but still counted among the masterpieces of Japanese romantic literature, was completed after some years' effort. Noteworthy novels, written by new writers who were to represent the coming age, also came out, including *Jûemon no Saigo* (The End of Ju-emon) by Katai, *Kyûshujin* (Former Master) by Tôson, *Shuchû Nikki* (Drinker's Diary) by Doppo and *Shunkô* (Spring Light) by Shûsei.

In addition to Zola, other western writers, for instance, Turgenev, though Futabatei's translations, and Nietzsche, introduced by Chogyû in his above-mentioned essays—had a big influence on the writers of the day.

Oguri Fûyô was in a sense a novelist representing this tendency. He was born in 1875 in Aichi Prefecture and was a disciple of Kôyô's from the time he was 18. He became recognized as a promising writer with the publication of *Neoshiroi* (Powdering at Night) and *Bekkôzuru* (Tortoise-shell Crane). After that he wrote many diverse works and gradually built himself up as a talented writer. The above-mentioned *Sametaru Onna* is indicative of his later long work *Seishun* (Youth), written in 1905. By nature, he was a skillful writer with an unusual capacity for imitating. While Tengai concentrated on assimilating Zola alone, he skillfully combined Zola, Turgenev and other western novelists and described the customs and psychology of the new era. In *Sametaru Onna,* for instance, he used the plot of Goethe's *Sorrows of Young Werther.* This kind of skill, however, is too often accompanied by lack of depth of understanding. Hisayo, the heroine of *Sametaru Onna,* and Tobari, the man she loved, seem very stiff and artificial. The commonplace Niwa's remarks seem more vivid and give the impression that the author's sympathies are more with him. Fûyô often depicts "susceptible young men who do not believe in anything and are simply tossed about by the transitory, frivolous trends of the times," but he was unable to describe their inner beings with any sympathy. This shortcoming is manifest in *Seishun,* the most gaudy display of his talent.

Another type of novel important in this period is the social novel—first advocated and written by Uchida Roan, Tokutomi Roka, Gotô

Chûgai, and further developed by Kinoshita Naoe. Its earliest advocate was Roan, who entered the literary world after being deeply moved by Dostoevsky's *Crime and Punishment*. At first he was active as a critic. He then came out with a translation of *Crime and Punishment*. In 1898 he published *Kure no Nijûhachinichi* (The 28th of December), his first attempt at the social novel he had been advocating. He had long felt strong dissatisfaction with the Kenyûsha-centered literary circle of the 1890's and called for a novel with sociological, historical meaning. Takayama Chogyû and Kaneko Chikusui's discussion on the social novel showed that people were finally ready for a social novel. It was thought that this favorable turn of tide spurred him to write *Kure no Nijuhachinichi*. The social novels of the day were far from our idea of a social novel; perhaps 'family novel' would be a better name for them. In Roan's above work, for example, *Ginnosuke,* a young man who planned to emigrate to Mexico to become a statesman, happened to marry into a rich family. Frequent clashes with his unsympathetic wife made his life miserable. At the advice of Shizue, a woman friend whom in his inner-heart he loved, he gave up his grand scheme of going to Mexico. In the eyes of the readers of his day who were fed up with *Kenyûsha* novels for their concentration on people 'madly in love, worn out from too much dissipation', this novel had a fresh appeal. It was highly praised by Tayama Katai and Masamune Hakuchô. In *Ukimakura* (The Life on the Waves), *Katauzura* (Separated Couple), *Rakkô* (Falling Red Petal) and *Shimokuzure* (Thawing Frost), he attempted to depict some of the real conditions of the society. This literary trend spread to other writer and stories about politicians came to be written. Gotô Chûgai wrote *Funikudan* (Group of Rotten Flesh, 1900) and Tokuda Shûsei, *Namakemono* (The Idler, 1899), both about politicians, while Oguri Fûyô described a politician's family life in *Seido* (Political Ass, 1899). But none of these stories were outstanding literary works. Consequently, the social novel movement—just like the ideological and tragic novel movements—came to be regarded as empty theory, unable to produce any concrete works of lasting value.

However, there was one novelist who was unusually popular with the public and who is still read today—Tokutomi Roka.

Roka (real name; Kenjirô) was born in the first year of Meiji, 1868, in Minamata, Kyushu. He started his literary career by writing for the magazine Kokumin no Tomo (People's Friend) and the newspaper Kokumin Shimbun, both put out by his elder brother, Sohô (Iichirô), a journalist-critic. But his character did not match his political-minded brother's—the ideological and emotional gap between them grew wider and wider. He became a baptised Christian, later was completely taken with Tolstoy, and in his later years had a special religion of his own.

In 1898 and 1899, he won a reputation for himself with the novel *Hototogisu* (The Cuckoo) that came out in Kokumin Shimbun in 1898-9, and in 1900 he surprised the world with the descriptions of nature depicted with the fresh sentiment of someone influenced by Christianity in *Shizen to Jinsei* (Nature and Human Life), a collection of short stories, criticism and essays that had first been published in Kokumin Shimbun and elsewhere.

Omoide no Ki (Recollections) that came out in Kokumin Shimbun the same year was a description of the author's own childhood and youth in the manner of Dickens. The hero's young demands for individual freedom and the resulting tumultuous behavior were a little crude but went well with the free and easy style. The author's lenient view of human beings and tendency to jump at conclusions were softened by the humor that came from youth. He created a character-image of a very appealing young man, unusual in Meiji literature. His next work, *Kuroshio* (The Black Tide) was a social novel, entirely different from his last work. It dealt with the early Westernization of Japan, symbolized by Rokumei-kan, describing the political corruption and high-society life, through the eyes of its main character, Tôzaburô, a courageous ex-soldier in support of the Shogunate and now living in seclusion.

The writer had originally planned to make it a six-volume work dealing with the Westernization period that started around 1887 and going through the Sino-Japanese War, ended with the establishment of the Social Democratic Party in April, 1901. Unfortunately the novel ended after the first volume, partly because Roka and his brother became at odds with each other and Roka left Kokumin Shimbun. Even this one volume outclassed other social novels of the day and is still worth reading in spite of its somewhat old-fashioned techniques and style.

After that, in 1906, Roka travelled across Palestine and visited Tolstoy on his way back to Japan. In 1907 he started living in the country side in Chitose-mura, Tokyo, and published a record of his life there, *Mimizu no Tawagoto* (The Prattling of an Earthworm). He set out on a trip around the world in 1919, which he described in "From Japan to Japan" in 1920, and in 1924 the first volume of *Fuji,* an autobiography which he and his wife wrote together. He continued to be active in his old age, but drifted away from the main literary currents. The personality quirk he had had since childhood grew more dominant and he led a more and more isolated life. He ended his life as a typical side-current writer—with a limited number of admirers and a diverse group of readers outside the literary world. In this respect his fate was similar to Izumi Kyôka, another great talent of the same period —although they were almost the opposite in character and style of writing. Both of them were more eccentric and strong willed than most other Japanese authors and both had a wide range of literary abilities. Perhaps over-production in Kyôka's case and under-production in Roka's isolated them from the literary activities of their day.

As the very fact that Roka dealt with it in his *Kuroshio* indicates, the establishment of the Social Democratic Party in May, 1901, by such men like Abe Isoo, Katayama Sen, Kinoshita Naoe, Kôtoku Denjiro (Shûsui), Kawakami Kiyoshi and Nishikawa Kôjiro, was an important event in the history of thought in this country. Though the party itself was immediately banned, the event showed that socialism was finally beginning to become a strong force in the Japanese world of thought. Right after the disbandment of the party, Kôtoku Shûsui riled Interior Minister Suematsu Kenchô, saying that the government could prohibit a socialistic political party, but that it would never be able to suppress socialistic thought itself. He said, "It is remarkable how increasingly powerful is becoming the socialistic thought in Japan, first studied and promulgated by scholars. Discouraged by the recent corruption of society, distressed by the economic confusion, people are trying to find a way out of the difficulties by extending full support to this system of thought."

It was only natural that in such an atmosphere, the above-mentioned advocacy of the social novel would lead to the birth of a more full-fledged socialistic novel.

It is no mere coincidence that Kinoshita Naoe, one of the representative writers of the socialistic novel in the Meiji period, happened to be one of the founders of the Social Democratic Party.

Kinoshita Naoe was born in 1869, as the son of a low-class Samurai of the Matsumoto Clan in Nagano Prefecture. Graduating from Tokyo Semmon Gakko, the predecessor of Waseda University, he became a lawyer at the age of 20, and as a Christian took an active part in moves against the prostitution system and the copper poisoning case at the Ashio Copper Mine. After taking part in the establishment of the Social Democratic Party, he helped out the Heimin (Commoner) Shimbun and wrote anti-war articles during the Russo-Japanese War. As in the case with Abe Isoo and Ishikawa Sanshirô, Naoe's socialistic thought was strongly influenced by Christian humanism, and in that respect, different from the non-religious, materialistic socialism of Kôtoku, Sakai (Kosen) and Katayama, which was better received by the Japanese. Possibly for this reason, Naoe left socialism, then the Christian faith too, in his later years and died in November, 1936, in the process of seeking enlightenment through Buddhism.

Two works, *Hi no Hashira* (Pillar of Fire, 1904) and *Otto no Kokuhaku* (Confessions of a Husband), which he wrote "in memory of the Russo-Japanese War," were not only important as forerunners of the Japanese socialistic novel, but also as novels that caused considerable repercussions among the readers.

Hi no Hashira and *Otto no Kokuhaku* both described the heroes who embody the ideals of the author, struggle with social evils. The former centered around the editor in chief of a Christian socialist newspaper, describing military and political bosses and government-patronized merchants. It also included exciting political events like coal miners' strikes and pacifist lecture meetings. At the same time it had elements of plot reminiscent of the political novels of the previous period, such as the daughter of a government-patronized merchant having an attachment for the hero. The feelings of its characters were exaggerated and while the work was certainly a full-fledged socialistic novel, it had something of the shallowness of a melodrama or *Sôshi Shibai* (political enthusiasists' play in the Meiji period).

Otto no Kokuhaku, on the other hand, elaborated on the conflicts between the hero, a Christian-humanist lawyer, and the conventional customs and habits of the farming society in Matsumoto, the author's native town. The novel is similar in theme to the works of Tengai and Fûyô, and better as a novel than *Hi no Hashira* in that the treatment of the characters was less forced and that it was written in a more flexible colloquial style. The fact that it came in a series of four in the *Mainichi Shimbun* between the summer of 1904 and 1906 was indicative of the good reception it got.

CHAPTER IX

Characteristics of Naturalism and
Its Pioneer Kunikida Doppo

As has been stated in various contexts, the naturalistic movement played an important part in the development of the modern novel, especially in Japan. One of the characteristic features of Meiji and Taisho literature is the important position held by the novel, and of the novel, in turn, the incomparably great importance of the naturalistic movement to it.

It was at this time that the novel became an established and conscious expression of modern thought in this country. The naturalistic influence was especially significant in that it was the theory behind later literary developments.

The golden age of naturalism in the literary world was at the longest four to five years, and maybe as short as one or two years. This shows the rapidity of up-and-down trends, a characteristic cultural phenomenon in modern Japan. Naturalistic and anti-naturalistic waves of thought appeared almost simultaneously, overlapping each other. When an anti-naturalistic system of thought—like symbolism or estheticism—once entered Japan it was interpreted in terms of naturalism, so naturalism and antinaturalism were two sides of the same trend of thought. Arthur Symon's famous *The Symbolistic Movements in Literature* was translated by Iwano Hômei, while Kitahara Hakushû said something to the following effect in his "Outline of the Development of Poetry in Meiji and Taisho Periods:" "It was when symbolic poetry was being transplanted to Japan that the thought of the French decadent poets also fascinated the young Japanese poetical world. Around the same time the naturalistic current also was raising its voice against conventional customs and thought. These two currents of thought were strangely united into one stream in the Japanese poetic world."

The driving force behind the trend of thought of the last decade of Meiji—which we might term the birth of self-awareness in modern literature—was naturalism. Writers who seemed to be in conflict with naturalism like the aesthetes, the new Shirakaba group writers, and even the lone giants like Ôgai and Sôseki actually used naturalism as a foundation—developing on it, revising it, or perfecting it.

There are many reasons for the huge influence the naturalism movement in our country had on society and later literature. We could outline its specific nature as follows.

1. It was a literature that was not merely influenced by European and Russian literature but actually formed from it, or at least the writers prided themselves in thinking so.

2. As a result, the gap between their literature and literature of earlier periods extended beyond a mere difference in schools—it was revolutionary or at least the writers' consciences asserted as much.

3. In substance, however, it was a perfected form or a special standardization of the romantic movement which had budded in the preceding period. It was based on an idealism aiming at liberation of everyone through personal liberation of the individual writer.

4. It was similiar to French naturalism in its strong spirit of opposition to and denial of 'power,' 'illusion' and so forth, the influence of scientific thought. But in this country the destruction movement even reached novels as a literary form causing a thorough blending of reality and truth.

5. For these two reasons (3 and 4), the novel written in the first person became an important literary form. It was on the one hand a writer's most direct means of self-expression, and on the other the novel-form closest to 'reality.'

6. Because of the feeling that 'artistry' in a novel was unnecessary or should be kept to a minimum there was a reformation in style. After that, novels were for the most part written in the vernacular.

7. Because of these characteristics of the movement, writers on the one hand kept pace with the trends of the times and at the same time set up their own special society called a 'literary world,' writing only for a limited number of readers and often for members of their own group.

These elements, although contradictory in a way, also blend with each other to form the 'mood' of an actual age. They appear in various combinations and nuances in the lives and works of the writers who represented naturalism.

Kosugi Tengai, Nagai Kafû and Oguri Fûyô have already been mentioned for the roles they played in paving the way for naturalism. But the most important forerunner of naturalism was Kunikida Doppo. He was not even fully conscious of the role he was playing, and his short life came to an end when the movement was at its height.

His real name was Tetsuo. He was born in the city of Chôshi in Chiba Prefecture in 1871 and grew up in Yamaguchi Prefecture. He came to Tokyo in 1887 and entered Tokyo Semmon Gakko (which later became Waseda University). He was baptised by Uemura Masahisa. In 1891 he quit school after being involved in a student riot, returned to Yamaguchi Prefecture, where he opened a private school. In 1893 he came back to Tokyo and became a newspaper reporter. The following year he went to Saeki in Ôita Prefecture and became principal of a private school, Tsuruya-Gakkan. It was then and there that his romantic poetic feelings were first aroused. With the outbreak of the Sino-Japanese War, he became a war correspondent for Kokumin Shimbun and gained a reputation with Aitei Tsûshin (Letters to My Dear Brother), reports in the form of letters addressed to his younger brother, sent from the warship, Chiyoda. After that he became a reporter of the magazine, Kokumin no Tomo, had a love affair with Sasaki Nobuko whom Arishima Takeo later based his novel Aru Onna (A Certain Woman), and married her despite the opposition of his friends. But she soon betrayed him, and the mental anguish left a mark on his works.

In his childhood he had idolized Yoshida Shôin and his ambition was to becom a politician. Christianity and the Minyûsha (publisher of Kokumin Shimbun and Kokumin no Tomo) bore strong environmental influences on him. With this background it was natural that his attitude toward literature was different from that of the Kenyûsha group, and also that his literary activities—although he followed Tôkoku's footsteps—were different from the Bungaku-kai group.

The influence of English literature and Christianity made him aware of the problems of life and made him desire, above all, to be a whole human being.

For a long time he was unable to choose between a political and a literary career, but finally he decided on becoming a 'teacher,' in the true sense of the word, making a profession of 'criticizing human life,' and chose literature as a tool to put this idea into practice. To him literature was hearing 'the natural voice of humanity' and teaching the world of 'the truth about love, sincerity and physical labor.'

Such a view of literature was certainly a new, unusual thing in the Kenyûsha-centered literary world of the day, which explains his long obscurity and also the central position in a new literary movement he suddenly occupied in his later years. As he himself said, the way I started writing novels was in a style and with a philosophy and treatment of characters that had almost no connection with my literary activity up to that time and was not influenced by Tokugawa literature or Kôyô and Rohan . . ."

When he asked himself the source of his literature, he answered 'Wordsworth,' and it was true that he started his literary career as a romantic poet, turning out his *Doppo Gin* (Doppo Recites a Poem) in *Jojô-shi* (Lyric Poetry), an anthology he writes with Tayama Katai and Matsuoka Kunio in 1897. Then in 1898 his *Musashi no* (Musashi Plain) and *Shikagari* (Deer Hunting), works very close to prose-poems, came out.

Typical of a pioneering writer of a transitional period, Doppo showed several style changes during his short life-time. During his first period, lasting until about 1900, he freely displayed his lyric-poet qualities, riding high on a wave of youthful emotion. The romantic poet Doppo in a sense, followed in the footsteps of Tôkoku, but his prose-poem like novels belong to the same family as Saganoya Omuro and Miyazaki Koshoshi's works and show the influence of Futabatei's *Aibiki* and *Meguriai.*

Like Futabatei and Tôkoku he was an idealist of a sort, whose art was born out of his painful quest of the meaning of literature, life and of art in human life. However, because he lived longer and in a later period than Tôkoku, he had a more complex mind and more realistic character.

"Doppo had a keen mind, and at the same time a gentle heart. But unfortunately they were at odds with each other, which was tragic for him." Akutagawa Ryûnosuke wrote in his essay 'Bungeiteki na Amarini Bungeiteki na,'' (Literary, too Literary). Doppo's uniqueness lies in that he could produce a fresh individualistic expression by frankly facing this conflict within himself. "Because of his sharp mind he couldn't help but look down at the earth, but because of his gentle heart he couldn't help but look up to heaven" Akutagawa continues. But his romantic stage, when he looked up to 'Heaven' soon ended, followed by the period of looking down at the 'earth' and the accompanying painful struggle.

There was a certain ambitious tendency or something of the speculator in Doppo as indicated by his trying his hand at a money-making scheme and failing. But the trend of the times was also at work here.

The ten years between the Sino-Japanese War and the Russo-Japanese War was a time when the desirability of worldly ambition was unquestionably accepted by the young people of the new age. It was a time when personal ambition and idealism could coexist without causing conflict. Doppo, as a child of the times, had strong ambitions to succeed in business enterprises and other worldly affairs but on the other hand he 'believed in his ideals' and saw 'criticism of human life' as his heavenly mission. This inner conflict or 'tragedy' wore him out both mentally and physically and deprived him of his life before he was forty. But because he was in the special position of living with the tide of the times and yet conscious of the emptiness of such a life, we might say that Doppo is the firstmodern Japanese poet to express in a novel the emptiness of the innerlife of the Meiji society which he felt in his own life.

In many of the works written after 1901, during his second period, his characteristics emerged very clearly. They are diverse in subject matter, but the characteristics common to all his representative works like Gyûniku to Bareisho (Beef and Potatoes, 1901), Tomioka Sensei (Professor

Tomioka), *Shuchû Nikki* (Drinker's Diary), *Unmeironsha* (The Fatalist) and *Junsa* (The Policeman) in 1902, and *Jonan* (Women Trouble) and *Shôjikimono* (Honest Fellow) in 1903. Many of them depict the sorrow of people who got rolled in the dirt of the world or were defeated people who were hurt because of their goodness. This characteristic became even more conspicuous in the naturalistic works of his third period. This period started around 1907, the year before his death. Fighting declining health, Doppo wrote during this short period short novels *Kyûshi* (Death in Poverty), *Nami no Oto* (The Sound of the Waves) and *Gôgai* (Extra) in 1907 and *Take no Kido* (Bamboo Door) and *Ni-Rôjin* (Two Old Men) in 1908. In these works he described calmly the little tragicomedies in the lives of common men. Of all Doppo's works (for that matter of all naturalistic short stories) these are the most perfect as literary works.

However, some of these works are in fact more indicative of the author's fatigue than his maturity. It was in the works of his second period and before his health declined when there was inner harmony of thought, action and art, that his individuality best came out. Some of his best short stories in this third period suggest not only his existence as a pioneer of naturalism but also the remains of his frustration as a rare romantic poet who was unable to express his poetic spirit to the fullest extent.

It is interesting that along with Doppo, Akutagawa named Futabatei and Takuboku as writers who lived 'tragic' lives. If we add Tôkoku we can categorize them as a romantic stream completely different from the main stream romanticism which Tekkan and Chogyû represented, unostentatious and consequently unable to gain popularity in their day, and yet devoting itself to freeing man's spirits.

"My deepest desire is to wake out of sleep, to shake off my dreams, to look straight at this strange, boundless universe and life in this universe. To find my naked self in this strange universe. Not merely to know about the strangeness, but to feel keenly the strangeness. Not to know about the secret of death, but to stand in awe of the reality of death. Not to gain faith, but to feel the fearful reality of this universe as it is, to such an extent that I cannot have even a moment's peace of mind without believing," writes Doppo in his *Okamoto no Techô* (Okamoto's Notebook).

Never in the history of this country had a romantic feeling, which led the human desire for freedom to the loneliness of coming face-to-face with the absolute, been expressed with such strong feeling. Doppo continued, "My desire is to always live, feeling this strong and deep emotion." And if this was the way he wanted his life to be, then his inner life was supported by far higher ambition than the works he left indicate.

But it was not only his works. Naturalistic writers who followed him also looked squarely at figures of humans who were 'afflicted by a desire for fame and caught by the desires of the flesh' and tried hard to describe them. But no writer appeared who could depict the fearful realities of this universe to an extent that one 'cannot get even a moment's peace of mind without having faith.'

"—Of course Doppo was a born poet . . . But he was a poet different from Mr. Shimazaki Tôson or Mr. Tayama Katai. We can't find anything like Mr. Tayama's poems which give the feeling of a wide river, or Mr. Shimazaki's which are like a field of flowers. His poetry is more tense. As he said in one of his poems, Doppo was always calling out 'Oh cloud up there on you Lofty Peak !' . . . Naturalistic novelists all struggled their way on their feet. But only Doppo soared up into the air once in a while."

Akutagawa Ryûnosuke, who ended his essay, "Kunikida Doppo," with the above words, is another author who destroyed himself by "soaring up in the air."

CHAPTER X

Katai, Tôson, Hômei and Shûsei

In the preface to his second work, *"Doppo-shû,"* Doppo wrote the following: "Like anyone else, I would like my works to be popular with the current reading public, but unfortunately, so far, not one of my works has become popular. Compared to the popular writers of the day, it seems as though I am sitting in a far corner of the literary scene."

He wrote this in July, 1906. When he died three years later, in June, 1909, he was the center of popularity. This was because during that short period there was an unprecedented literary revolution in this country—specifically, the ascendency of naturalism.

Naturalistic thought was first introduced to Japan in 1889 when Mori Ôgai discussed Zola in his *"A View of the Novel Based on Medical Theory."* As was already mentioned, this way of thinking gained the sympathy of young people in the fourth decade of Meiji (1897–1906) for its aim of breaking conventional social customs, and was gradually understood more widely and deeply through the efforts of Tengai, Fûyô, Kafû, Katai and Tôson.

In France and other countries where its naturalism and the scientific thought were a reaction against Romanticism and its essence—liberation of human feelings. In Japan, however, one of the main features of naturalism was that it was one phase of Romanticism that later on served to perfect romanticism. Shimamura Hôgetsu, in his *"Naturalism in Literature"* cites Rousseau in France as a forerunner of naturalism. This is only natural since the concept of individual freedom arose as a result of the influence of science-centered Western culture that came into Japan then.

But few people seem to notice that this resulted in the unique form of the novel written in the first person.

Tayama Katai explained in the preface to his *No no Hana* (Flowers in the Field), 1901, the importance of a writer's getting away from his own 'trivial subjectivity,' portraying 'an image of Nature' and showing 'human inclination.' By the term 'a writer's trivial subjectivity' he meant conventional morality that controls a writer's mind and literary devices used for vulgar appeal. In his famous essay, *"Open Description"* written in 1904, he developed this thesis. He said that in the East and West alike all literature before the first half of the 19th century was 'gilted' and that a characteristic feature of 'Western literature after the 19th Century revolution' was the tearing down of this 'gilted' literature. "The outcry 'everything must be outspoken, true, natural' echoed to every corner of the Continent. If you think it's a lie, look at Ibsen, look at Zola, look at Dostoyevsky. What blood and sweat we can find in their works!"

We should take note that the word 'natural' here is used almost synonymously with 'frank' and 'true.' Doppo too used the word 'natural' to refer to the concept opposite to established social order (which of course included established art forms). ". . . I cannot think of man as something apart from nature. The life of a common man in commonplace circumstances becomes a vital reality only as a part of the beautiful, mysterious world of nature, which is in accord with man." (*"Wordsworth's Naturalism and Myself"*) If we look at these words of Doppo's along with Katai's we can see, above the subtle, individual differences, an overall system of thought of an age maturing.

Katai's *Jûemon no Saigo* (1902) is an expression of this system of thought. Also prominent in Shimazaki Tôson's *Hakai* (Breaking an Oath, 1906) an epoch-making novel that was the first to put the tenets of naturalism into a concrete form, were Doppo's ideas or the thinking of his times which influenced all new writers but was most highly formulated by Doppo.

Almost needless to say, *Hakai* was received by the literary world of the day, especially by young people who were to make up the future literary world, as a fresh new literary work in every sense of the word. A number of historians have already explained that the novel's uniqueness was the result of Tôson's nearly ten years of lone studying and disciplining himself. Toson's *Hakai* met the demands of his age in many respects. I would like to explain briefly in what respects the novel met the demands of the age.

Hakai is a novel which borrowed heavily from *"Crime and Punishment,"* all the way from its theme to the treatment of the characters. But Tôson chose as the scene of his work a country town in central Japan instead of the urban, city environment of his model. Undoubtedly part of the reason was that he tried to make use of the 'studies' of nature he had made of the rural town of Komoro while he was there. But considering the fact that *Hakai* was a novel upon which the writer risked his literary life, a more essential reason for choosing this 'local' scene must have been the thought of the times as Doppo himself said; "What is the history of the family living in this cottage by the river? What is that old man's background? Look at that stone. Doesn't it commemorate a tender human feeling? Isn't it more meaningful than a tall monument in a city?—Here is a record of nature, human feelings and god. This is a place which has witnessed the life and death of numberless people, men and women, and their souls. To learn about Caesar's life is to become Caesar and to see this world the way he did. Is the same thing not required in learning about that farmer? I am a child of knowledge. This farmer is a child of a mountain village and the fields—We city people want to get inside the farmer and look at this world from there." *(Biography of a Common Man)*

In *Hakai* Tôson not only tried to get into Segawa Ushimatsu and to 'look at this world from there,' but also made a confession of his own inner life through Ushimatsu. It is here that Tôson's originality—which in a way rises above the age—lies, as will be discussed later. The fact that his confession took the form of a novel in which its principal character, Ushimatsu, an outcaste, tried to keep his background secret, shows that Tôson, too, like Doppo, was influenced by Wordsworth and Ruskin.

We should call to mind here that Yanagida Kunio was among the poets who edited the anthology *Jojôshi* (Lyrical Poems) together with Doppo and Katai. He too believed that 'for the true history of the human race we must ask the common people living in the mountain and fishing villages,' and he spent half his life investigating the 'record of nature, human feelings and god,' building the foundation for the study of Japanese folk lore. The subject matter of *Hakai* was partly a product of the fashions of the day and the same can be said for the style.

The opening sentence of *Hakai*, "Rengeji dewa geshuku o kaneta" (The Rengeji Temple took in boarders) gave a fresh impression to 20 year-olds of the day, as Satomi Ton says, but at the same time repulsed influencial editors like Takita Choin. His colloquial sentence style which avoided as much as possible flowery expressions was something that Doppo had learned from Wordsworth and already used. Katai, too, held as his ideal 'the more vulgar the subject matter is, the more down-to-earth-the style grows; the more out-spoken the idea, the more outspoken the style.'

Hakai should not be undervalued for what has been said so far. An artist's primary mission is to put into a concrete form the unformulated thinking and feelings shared by the people of one age. The most unique quality of this novel, is not that it is a mere social novel or novel dealing with a social problem, but that Tôson created Ushimatsu not simply objectively as an outcast elementary school teacher but as a human being with an inner life closely linked with the author's own flesh and blood.

Of course these are not strictly speaking two separate things. For a character to really touch a chord in a reader's heart, and arouse true sympathy, he must be portrayed not only as a social (external) being but with an inner self. Doppo instinctively knew this. It is impossible to describe a character's inner life without the writer's exposing his own inner self.

When Tôson, through Ushimatsu, confessed the 'secrets' lying 'deep in his own heart,' he succeeded in creating in Ushimatsu a living character with psychological depth, something neither Doppo nor Katai were able to do.

Just as the cheracter Bunzo in *Ukigumo* is the writer, Futabatei, himself, Ushimatsu is Tôson himself. In this respect *Hakai* is *Ukigumo*'s successor.

Probably this explains why Shimamura Hôgetsu termed the novel "a summing up of various predecessors, a bright banner of a new current," and praised it "Japanese fiction has finally created a work which equals, and shares its life with, the controversial works of the modern school of European naturalism."

The appearance of this novel indicated that in Tôson as well as in all fiction writers of Japan, the time was ripe for the birth of the modern novel. For instance, taking two other novels that appeared in 1906—Natsume Sôseki's *Wagahai wa Neko de aru* (I am a Cat) and Futabatei's *Sono Omokage* (The Image)—the authors created a new individualistic form of literature by borrowing the novel form to make their own confessions.

This period was like a second daybreak in the history of the modern Japanese novel, comparable to the period around 1887. The dawn actually came the following year with the publication of Tayama Katai's *Futon*. As a result of his work a special novel-form called the 'I' novel or the novel written in first person, where fictional structure is ignored and the author appears directly in the novel to confess his inner thoughts—is raised to the position of the main current of novel. I have discussed the details in my *"Essay on Popular Novels."* Since I may have over-estimated the importance of *Futon's* role, however, I want to consider here the reasons why *Futon* stimulated such a rapid popularization of the 'I' novel.

First, as I said before, in this country the naturalistic movement itself played the same role as the romantic movement did in Europe. Although the writers of the day were not fully aware of it, they regarded writers of the romantic school as no more than forerunners of naturalism. For instance, Hôgetsu said in his essay which I quoted earlier. "The naturalism of Rousseau and Wordsworth was at the same time a type of romanticism. From the very beginning, romanticism contained naturalism."

Earlier I touched on how liberation of human feelings, respect for inner-man above the external norms of society and other values established by European romanticism climbed into the writers' consciousness as nature in this country with its negligible Romantic movement. Hôgetsu's words above are a good illustration of the process. (Takuboku, too, in his *"The Current StAge op-gap"* agreed with his opponent Uozumi Setsuro that Japanese naturalism was characterized by being a combination of the two mutually opposed ideas of self-assertion and self-negation.)

We should also remember that Tôson, Katai, Doppo and Hômei—the leading naturalistic writers—were all romantic poets. The Japanese naturalistic movement was fundamentally a successor of romanticism. It was carried on by romantic poets themselves as a reaction to the romantic school but also as the consummation of the metamorphosis of their earlier work.

As a result, in this shifting from poet to prose writer lies the essence of the naturalistic movement. The common phrase that applies to their metamorphosis is 'from fancy to reality.'

"Is this a poet's empty dream? No, it's reality," Doppo said in *Bonjin no Den*. This tendency to look for support for one's own isolated ideas in the realities of the external world is also very conspicuous in Tôson at the time when he first turned to writing fiction. Usui Yoshimi says "Tôson had been aiming at the same goal ever since he wrote *Wakana-shû*. But he had to borrow from others even the minutest details of character description." *(Dispute on the Model Problem)* He went on to closely analyze the way Tôson in his early works, under the strong influence of Rousseau's 'Confessions,' took his plots from *Madame Bovary, The Doll House* and *Crime and Punishment,* and how he made an unusual self-confession while taking even the most minute details of character description from others. This reflects a natural maturing process—where a poet no longer able to believe in the 'empty dreams' of his youth tries to express his inner world through 'reality.' It also indicates his struggles as an artist.

A defect of Tôson's early works seems to have derived from the dilemma in his attempt to support fiction with a set of accumulated, naked 'facts.' Be that as it may, if a regard for 'realities' can be combined with the above-mentioned romantic concept of 'nature,' and if 'confessions' can attract authors in a new direction (because of the under-developed romantic literature), then the simplest and most appropriate way to fulfil the literary demands of the age is for the author to see himself as 'nature,' and 'confess' the 'realities' in his own life as they are. This was exactly the answer Katai found in his *Futon*.

The just criticism, that making the novel a place to confess the author's private life, robs the novel of its very life-blood, or its fictional quality, and will eventually turn it into an artistic autobiography or diary, failed to deter 'I' novels from emerging as the new main current of literature in Japan. After *Futon* (1907), Tôson's *Haru* (Spring, 1908) and *Ie* (Family, 1910), Hômei's *Tandeki* (Indulgence, 1909) and *Hôrô* (Wandering, 1910), Shûsei's *Kabi* (Mold, 1911), and Katai's next works, *Sei* (Life, 1908) and *Tsuma* (Wife, 1909) came out in succession.

The popularity of the 'I' novels was demonstrative of just how fascinating were the images of the 'poet' expressed through the 'realities' of life to the readers of the day. Of course, these 'poets' claimed to be 'common, everyday men,' but it is obvious to readers today that the heroes of all these novels (often paradoxically described) were idealists or seekers after truth of a sort.

Thus, a peculiar situation was formed in Japan with the personal confessions of poets who discarded all empty dreams and only wrote 'realities,' regarded not only as novels, but also as the basic form of novel. Perhaps the reason behind this trend was the excessive faith that all of the Meiji people had in 'facts' and 'science,' traceable to the enthusiasm for 'civilization and enlightenment.' The national feeling was described by Kanagaki Robun, who said, "With knowledge increasing from month to month and day to day, people have come to look down on novels as falsehoods and delusions."

Japan was no different from France, in that the naturalistic movement was born out of an atmosphere of scientific thought of the days. However, there is naturally a difference between the people who gave birth to the scientific way of thinking of its own and people who first encountered science in the form of the foreign 'black ship,' railways and telecommunications, and who found out about science by external imitation, and experienced a revolutionary change in their lives. I cannot discuss this fully here, but, in a nutshell, the word 'science' had a far more magical power in Japan than in its place of origin, Europe. At the same time, however, it had no substantial influence on people's thinking.

In Japan, too, natural science and the rationalism behind it shook the existing moral code based on traditional authority, and called up an age of scepticism and disillusionment among sensitive men with strong conscience. However, it did not bring about an effort to build a new system of thought and ethics to replace the old.

"Some people wonder why Japanese naturalism could not produce more powerful works, but they should realize that it was not literary forces alone that produced works like Balzac's that are like lofty stone structures. We should remember that the power of French science— Pasteur's bacteriology and Poincaré's mathematics and astronomy—lay behind those literary works," Shimazaki Tôson said. What this country really lacked was not 'science' but the efforts of a Comte and Taine to construct a science-based system of thought.

The destructive influence of science upon the human mind was, then, limited in Japan to a group of intellectuals, and did not spread to society in general. Those who were enlightened to 'modern thought,' had a paradoxical pride in being the conscience of the age by living in disillusionment and scepticism. The confessional novel, with the author himself as the hero, was the most natural form of expression for those romantic poets fascinated by the spirit of positivism. It was no wonder that those poets who tried to impress their readers by the force of 'realities' regarded the fictional aspect of a novel as a nuisance to be eliminated.

As a result, a writer, when he took material for a novel from outside his personal experiences, was censured for writing 'plated' literature with 'frivolous elements.' As I mentioned before, the 'I' novel, in spite of its almost fatal shortcomings as a novel, immediately became the mainstay of literature of the age, its influence still being felt today. It was a style best answering the author's demands for self liberation and best fitted to the characteristic spirit of the age, a spirit of rationalism, which was superficial, and yet for that very reason, outwardly rigid. In this respect, *Futon* was something more than epoch-making. It was a fate-determining work, which decided the direction of the modern Japanese novel. It's author, Tayama Katai, is a man we can never forget in this respect.

Tayama Katai (his real name: Rokuya) was born in 1871 in Tatebayashi, Gumma Prefecture. He came to Tokyo at a young age to help support his family, and soon became interested in literature under the influence of his elder brother. Since his youth, he associated with members of the Kenyûsha, published practice novels through that organization, helped published the above-mentioned *Jojôshi,* and wrote a number of travelogues. He also associated with writers like Tôson and Doppo, read foreign literary works, and came to be known by a segment of the population for his short novels, *No no Hana* (Flowers in the Field) and *Jûemon no Saigo* (The End of Jûemon).

But it was *Futon,* as mentioned before, that won him fame, making him one of the representative naturalistic authors of the day. In this work, he wrote of his actual love affair with a young woman literary follower who stayed with his family. The novel shocked the readers for its bold exposure of the writer's life, and as the confession of a middle-aged man, with fleshly appetites. He then established his position as an author of the 'I' novel with the publication of a trilogy, *Sei* (Life, 1908), *Tsuma* (Wife, 1909) and *En* (Relation, 1910), and broadened his scope with *Inaka Kyôshi* (Country Teacher), which was termed an 'objective novel,' in which he wrote a sympathetic portrayal of the brief life of a country elementary-school teacher in poor health. As a pioneer of naturalism, Katai had both good points and shortcomings. When the relatively short-lived prime period of naturalism was over, he suffered the most artistic agony of any of his friends. Japanese naturalism —that strange combination of rationalism and romanticism—was inconsistent within itself. For the writer there was a basic conflict between his job as a writer of describing his life just as it was in its inconclusive state, as 'nature experienced and observed by himself,' and his indispensable moral requirement as a human being to work out somehow a solution for his life. This is an involved problem concerning art and life; it can never be settled within the realm of literature alone.

Katai had so deep an affection for literature throughout his life, that few other writers can equal him in the selflessness of that affection. Perhaps it was for this reason that his naturalistic theories were limited to literary opinions. The impasse he came to in his life resulted from the overly literary nature of his naturalistic theories. In the Taishô Period (which began in 1912), Katai grew increasingly interested in religion; had a sympathy for writers like Huysmans, who was converted from naturalism to Catholicism; and wrote essays and novels like *Hitonigiri no Wara* (A Handful of Straw, 1914), *Sansô ni Hitori Ite* (Staying Alone at a Mountain Cottage 1916), *Aru Sô no Kiseki* (A Monk's Miracle, 1917) and *Zansetsu* (Patches of Snow, 1917) and two long works expressing a kind of transientism, *Toki wa Sugiyuku* (Time Goes By, 1916), and *Futatabi Kusa no No ni* (Revisiting a Grassy Field, 1918). But his views on life and death and the rise and fall of man described in these works remained within sentimental romanticism, and seemed dated in the midst of the new Taisho literature that was the blossoming.

Though he published some excellent short stories like *Tabi no Mono* (The Traveler, 1916) and *Ippeisotsu no Jûsatsu* (The Soldier's Execution, 1917), on the whole his reputation declined. In his later years, he wrote *Minamoto no Yoshitomo*, 1924 and other historic novels, but they were unable to rekindle his past fame. His last work, an excellent one, *Hyaku-ya* (A Hundred Nights, 1927), was also virtually neglected at the time it came out.

In spite of his naturalistic theories, or rather shown by his so naive belief in just one literary theory, Katai was above all a sentimental and romantic poet throughout his life. His sentimentalism, which appeared in a raw form in his earlier works, passed through cruel theory and rich life experiences to come out uniquely and develop in his later years. The goodness of the writer's heart emerged in the novels and short stories he wrote toward the end of his life. With no thought or hope of impressing his readers, he wrote warmly of all phases of human life—himself included—fusing them all with nature.

When Tôson was called to Katai's death-bed, he is said to have asked Katai, in all seriousness, to tell him what man feels when he dies. This episode shows Tôson's attitude toward life, as well as giving us a glimpse into the basic nature of naturalism.

It was mentioned earlier that Tôson, unlike Katai, was a renowned poet. In temperament, however, he was more a moralist, than a romantic poet, who turned his sharp, observant eyes on himself and others in a desire to get to the essence of things. His switch to prose was an inevitable event in his maturing process. After becoming an established novelist with the publication of *Hakai,* he wrote one novel after another, such as *Haru* (Spring, 1908), *Ie* (1909), *Sakura no Mi no Jukusuru Toki* (When the Cherries are Ripe, 1914) and *Shinsei* (New Life, 1918), all of them winning extreme acclaims.

All of these works were in the form of the 'I' novel, belonging to the same literary current as Katai's *Futon,* but in contrast to Katai's basically appreciative attitude toward life, Tôson's works, which had a strong underlying desire for life that cries out, "Though I am worthless, I do want somehow to live!" were basically ethical. His confessions have complex dimensions, all the more so because elaborate artistic efforts were involved For Tôson, writing a poem was like 'Shipping' himself. In his novels too he described how he whipped himself; it looks as if he was trying to use those confessions as an excuse for life.

His works of this period are represented by *Ie* and *Shinsei.* The former depicts the decline of two old families of Kiso, one the Koizumis to whom the hero Sankichi, who has the author himself as a model, belonged, and the other the Hashimotos into which the hero's elder sister Otane had married. The latter, *Shinsei,* describes how the hero lost his wife, had an affair with his niece, went to France and returned to Japan three years later only to find himself falling back into his old relationship with the niece. It touched off a lot of criticism because this was the author's own confession—in the form of a novel—and so sudden that even his friends did not know about the love affair. "I have never seen a hypocrite as cunning as the hero of *Shinsei,*" said Akutagawa Ryûnosuke, while Masamune Hakuchô commented, "In this work, a man who was lost tries to describe the pains of being lost and the secret pleasures only known to the lost. It's wrong to expect salvation in life from this confessional literature."

By writing this novel, however, the author somehow came out of a crisis in his life. After that, he published such novels as *Arashi* (The Storm,

1926) and *Bunpai* (Sharing, 1927) dealing with his own children who grew up and became independent. In his later life, Toson put all his efforts into *Yoakemae* (Before Dawn, 1936), a lengthy work depicting the Japanese society around the time of the Meiji Restoration, centering on a Kiso street, with the author's father as the main character. A noticeable side of Tôson as a moralist was his criticism of modern civilization. His fervent 'I want to live' passion inevitably led him from a sincere desire to live a better life to a contact with and criticism of all aspects of his society. In this sense, Tôson was a persistent critic of his age but the object of his criticism was not simply the traditional customs and morality of the past but included the new unripened, imported culture.

"How annoying to have been born in this age . . . Why aren't we allowed to live our own lives to the fullest? It's understandable, I guess. Those Europeans came to their present level of social-life over a long period of time. We have only a short time to catch up with them." He wrote in *Iigura Dayori* (Letters from "Iigura"). These words sound the keynote of his criticism of modern civilization. This talent was something he inherited from Kitamura Tôkoku that grew more profound after his stay in France. On the surface his words sound mild, but the burning critical spirit underneath not only gives a special value to his *France Dayori* (Letters from France), *"L'Etranger"* and other travel essays but is also one of the most important reasons his works are read more widely and enthusiasticly today than any other work by naturalistic writers.

Tôson was a Christian for a time in his youth. Christianity, along with Tôkoku, bore strong influences in his life and thought. He was not the only one to be influenced by Christianity. The relationship between Christianity and literature became closer, especially in the case of writers between naturalism and the Shirakaba group. We can regard Doppo, Hakuchô and Naoya's novels as the literature of people who had left the church. Most characteristic among them was Iwano Hômei.

He should be numbered, along with Katai and Tôson, as one of the pioneers of naturalism. Like others, he was known as a poet between 1897 and 1906, the fourth decade of Meiji. His real name was Yoshie. He was born in Sumoto on Awaji Island in 1873 and from an early age sent to mission schools in Osaka and Tokyo. He was a faithful Christian and wanted to become a missionary. He soon became disillusioned by Christianity, but never lost the religious, educational zeal he had as a boy. Even when he was advocating naturalism and the nationalism he upheld later on, he always acted like an apostle. He had the pride and enthusiasm of an apostle to the end of his life.

In anthologies like *Tsuyujimo* (Dew and Frost, 1901), *Yûshio* (Evening Tide, 1904) *Hiren Hika* (Elegies on Sad Love, 1905) and *Kaiho Gishi* (Coast Battery Engineer, 1905), he excelled in long poems with an unusual way of thinking and wrote as a romantic poet opposed to the *Myôjô* group of romanticism. In 1906, he wrote *"Partial Animistic Mysticism"* and took the stand point that a phenomenon is real and nature is spiritual, advocating naturalistic symbolism, said, "The purpose of literature is to bring into play the bitter struggle between body and soul to gain momentary ascendancy over each other." After that he wrote one more collection of poems, *Yami no Haiban* (Wine Cup in the Dark, 1908), and then became a novelist. First he came out with *Tandeki* (Indulgence, 1909), which owes much to *Futon,* and then, out of his belief that 'art is action,' undertook a crab canning enterprise in Sakhalin, failed, and while wandering around Hokkaido, wrote a criticism *"Philosophy of Sorrowful Pains"* (1910) and collected materials for his later masterpiece, *Gobusaku* (A Five-part Work).

Gobusaku is a series of novels, *Hôrô* (Wandering), *Dankyô* (Broken Bridge), *Hatten* (Development), *Dokuyaku o Nomu Onna* (Woman Who Takes Poison), and *Tsukimono* (Obsession), written between 1910 and 1918. It was mainly about the relationship between Tamura Yoshio, the author himself, who failed in a canning enterprise and was loitering around Hokkaidô living off his friends, and Shimizu Otori, who chased after Yoshio like a woman possessed. After their love was ruptured there was almost a feeling of hatred between the two, and yet at an impasse in their lives they planned to commit a double suicide. In that the pathetic comedies of this 'behaviorist philosopher of momentarism,' are consistently described through the author's thorough subjectivity this is a complete 'I' novel. Unlike Tôson and Katai, however, Hômei not only used his way of thinking to interprete his own life, but he was also firmly convinced that he could build a new life on it. Going beyond the artistic limits of the usual 'I' novel, he did not hesitate to describe the sordid side of life. Through this naive intellectual attitude he made an impact on the readers which can almost be compared to that of Don Quixote. While this 'behaviorist philosopher' withstood the pains of life by indulging himself in thoughts, he was sensitive to every warm or cool glance others cast on him. The author's image in his actual life, undescribed in the novel, once in a while shows itself with striking clarity.

However, in order to feel this effect, which even the author himself was not expecting, a reader must have both an understanding and sympathy with the way of thinking of Hômei, and this, of course, cannot be expected of the general reader. In this sense, Hômei's *Gobusaku* must be criticised for an important artistic miscalculation and it was only natural that his reputation was limited in scope, when compared with that of his contemporaries like Tôson, Katai and Shûsei.

His theory that art is action, in essence, pertained to poetry rather than the aesthetics of the novel which must have more complex dimensions. His skill as a novelist came out more in short stories such as *Hito-ka Kumaka* (Man or Bear?, 1913), *Bonchi* (Young Master, 1914) and *Osei* (1919), than in the long work, *Gobusaku*. In his later years, he became interested in Shinto, advocated nationalism and made newspaper headlines with his family troubles. He died in 1921 at 47. This writer was exceptional as a naturalistic writer for his style and early death.

Tokuda Shûsei was a writer who, on the contrary to Hômei, never had any formulated way of thinking, and built up a unique way of expressing himself through a constant and conscious resistance to any 'solution' for life. The 'solution-free' attitude toward life is the aspect of naturalism strongly advocated by people like Hasegawa Tenkei, and in temperament Shûsei best represents naturalism of this type.

Unlike the other three writers, he did not start as a poet. He was a follower of other naturalistic writers rather than a pioneer, and eventually surpassed them.

Born in 1871 in Kanazawa, he became a disciple of Ozaki Kôyô early in his youth together with Kyôka, a friend from the same town, and established his fame as a novelist with *Kumo no Yukue* (Where the Clouds Go, 1900).

During the 4th decade of Meiji (1897–1906), he published a number of fairly good works and became known as one of the big-four followers of Kôyô along with Kyôka, Fûyô and Shunyô. During the Kenyûsha age, however, he did not attract much attention because of his unpretentious style. But when the age of naturalism came, the same plain realism fitted in with the new age, and he came to be watched as a naturalistic novelist with the publication of *Shinjotai* (The New Home) in 1908. It was a medium-length novel which gave a solid description of the hardships of the wife of a small businessman in the suburbs of Tokyo. Also influenced by the current trends of his age, Shûsei then turned to the 'I' novel, and wrote about his wife's life in *Ashiato* (Footprints, 1910) and about the circumstances of his marriage to her in *Kabi* (Mold, 1911). The figure of an obscure writer, Sasamura (the writer himself), who bore his lacklustre life by becoming apathetic, was minutely described as a symbol of the no-ideals, no-solution life. As a result, the novel became not only Shûsei's representative work, but a typical Japanese naturalistic 'I' novel.

Shûsei became a naturalist by letting his own inborn talents develop naturally rather than through theory. This nonchalant, most 'natural' naturalist of all, left works presenting the best of his talent and even the distinctiveness of a great writer, such as *Tadare* (The Sore, 1913) and *Arakure* (The Daredevils, 1915), during the period of decline of this literary school. His working pace slowed down for a while after 1916. But toward the end of the Taisho period, he resumed his activities as an 'I' novelist, prodded by the death of his wife and a love affair he had around that time, and gained a reputation by publishing many short stories describing his own life.

We should take note of the two masterpieces written in his later years, *Kasô Jinbutsu* (Men in Disguise, 1938), the balance sheet of his love affair, and his unfinished, last work, *Shukuzu* (The Epitome), which described the life of a Geisha. The two long novels were the height of Japanese naturalism, and were but also deeply respected by the young authors and critics of the time as two of the greatest modern Japanese novels.

The four writers above had all been active for a long time on the literary scene before the naturalistic age, spending their youth tasting the sorrows of forerunners and the pains of pioneers. But there were other fortunate writers who happened to meet this new current in their youth, who, in other words, met the harvesting period without experiencing the labor of the planting season. The expression of their fresh sensitivity, unspoiled by the 'old literature,' amazed the readers and senior writers of the day. It could not be denied, however, that their scale as writers was smaller than their predecessors.

The youngest and one with the most dazzling talent was Masamune Hakuchô (real name, Tadao). Born in a fishing village in Okayama Prefecture in 1879, he entered the Tokyo Semmon Gakko, became interested in Christianity under the influence of Uchimura Kanzô and was baptized by Uemura Masahisa in 1897.

Gradually, however, he became more interested in drama and literature than in Christianity, and left the church several years later. After publishing criticism and novels under the guidance of Shimamura Hôgetsu, he drew attention as a new naturalistic novelist with a short story, *Jin-Ai* (The Dust), which he submitted to the magazine *Shumi* (Taste) in 1907. He established his reputation with medium-length novels, *Doko-e* (Where To?), *Tamatsukiya* (Billiards Hall), *Satsuki-nobori* (May Streamer) and *Nikazoku* (Two Families) which he published one after another the following year.

Doko-e describes a typical youth of the new age and is regarded as the representative work of Hakuchô's early period. Its hero Kenji, depicted as an out-and-out nihilist who had lost interest in life, naturally gives the impression of being the author himself. Not only this one, but all his early novels were completely clear of romantic sentimentalism and traditional ethics, with the author taking an immoral, or more exactly, amoral view of life. They captured the minds of young people by giving an impression that the author had torn off a segment of life and flung it out in front of the readers.

Next he wrote excellent works like *Bikô* (Faint Light, 1910) and *Doro Ningyo* (Clay Doll, 1911), and became even more famous in the Taisho period, even after the wane of naturalism, with a description of the dark aspects of life, as in *Irie no Hotori* (By a Small Bay, 1915), *Ushibeya no Nioi* (Cattle Shed's Smell, 1916), *Hito Samazama* (Various Kinds of People, 1921) and *Umare-zarishi-naraba* (If One Had Not Been Born, 1923). After the Great Kanto Earthquake, he published modern and historic plays such as *Jinsei no Kôfuku* (Happiness in Life, 1924), *Azuchi no Haru* (Spring in Azuchi, 1926) and *Mitsuhide to Shôha* (1926). Between late Taisho and early Showa he wrote a number of critical biographical essays of contemporary writers, and later compiled them into *Bundan Jinbutsu Hyôron* (Critical Essays on Figures in the Literary World, 1932), in which he created a unique method of modern criticism by probing into the guiding principles of a writer's way of life through his works.

He made two trips abroad around that time and wrote some unique travelogues, and until after the war was active as a novelist and critic. He died in 1962, shortly after Kafû, who was the same age. As is widely known, he stayed amazingly young in spirit to the end of his long life, and his unusually flexible mind is thought to have come from his being a romantic poet at heart—a sensitive critical spirit wearing the mask of a realist.

Unlike Hakuchô, Mayama Seika (real name, Akira) had a brief and unfortunate career as a novelist. Born in 1878 in Sendai, he became a follower of Oguri Fûyô, and wrote a number of novels such as *Minami Koizumi Mura* (South Koizumi Village), a set of works which dealt with a farming village on the outskirts of Sendai, and for a while was as well known as a new naturalist writer as Hakuchô.

But he had to cut off his literary activities after the same manuscript was published simultaneously in two magazines, and did not come back on the literary scene until 1924 with the publication of a play, *Genboku to Chôei*.

Chikamatsu Shûkô (real name, Tokuda Kôji), born in 1876, came from the same town and was a classmate of Hakuchô's. He first gained recognition with his *Wakareta Tsuma ni Okuru Tegami* (Letters to My

Divorced Wife, 1910). Mainly he wrote 'I' novels with a strong tint of idealistic lyricism and he was a little outside the orthodox naturalistic tradition. He is known for openly confessing a man's psychological weakness. His set of works, *Kurokami* (Dark Hair, 1922) was a tribute to the burning love affair in his own life.

Kamitsukasa Shôken (real name, Nobutaka) was born in Nara in 1874. In 1911 after many years with Yomiuri Shimbun, he published *Mokuzô* (Wooden Statue), which had broad, social implications rare for a work by a naturalistic writer. His representative novel is *Hamo no Kawa* (The Sea Eel's Skin, 1914) which dealt with city life in the Kansai District. Shôken became acquainted with Sakai Toshihiko while he was still young, and since he had long been a newspaperman, many of his long novels had social implications. *Tokyo,* a long novel written in his later years, is the best example. The best of his works, however, are his sketches of city life and his 'I' novels. Among other minor naturalistic novelists were Mizuno Yôshû, Mishima Sôsen, Ikuta Kizan and Nakamura Seiko.

PART TWO

JAPANESE FICTION IN THE TAISHÔ ERA

(1912-1926)

A MEETING OF THE PAN SOCIETY

CHAPTER XI

Characteristics of the Taishô Period

One of the main features of the modern Japanese novel is the quick turn-over in trends, at least on the surface. This pertains not only to literature but Japanese modern culture in general. Even since the late Meiji period, a certain flurry was reflected in the history of novels—a restlessness like spring in the north country where suddenly plum, peach and cherry blossoms come out but summer comes so soon that people have little time to really look at the blossoms.

In the preceding chapter, I explained that naturalism had many things in common with aestheticism, which it later evolved into, and that they were merely two sides of the same system of thought. In 1908 and 1909 two of Nagai Kafû's works, *Amerika Monogatari* (The American Stories) and *Fransu Monogatari* (The French Stories) were published which were the forerunners of and became the foundation for aestheticism here. These two works had come out in magazines earlier, almost simultaneously with the early representative works of naturalism, such as *Futon* (The Quilt), *Sei* (Life), *Doko-e* (Where To?), *Haru* (Spring) and *Shinjotai* (The New Home).

The year 1909 was an important year in this respect. While famous naturalistic works or works influenced by naturalism—such as Hômei's *Tandeki* (Indulgence), Katai's *Inaka Kyôshi* (Country Teacher) and Ôgai's *Vita Sexualis* were written, novels with a completely different slant, including Sôseki's *Sorekara* (And Then) and Kafû's *Sumida-Gawa* (Sumida River) and *Kanraku* (Pleasure) were also attracting new readers. It was also in that year that the magazine *Subaru* (Pleiades) was established by young aesthetic writers, centered around Ôgai; The Pan Society, a gathering of aesthetic poets, was already in existence by then.

By the following year, 1910, the literary trends had already changed. Izumi Kyôka, who had kept a brief silence during the ascendency of naturalism, wrote *Uta Andon* (Song and the Lantern) for the January issue of the *Shin Shôsetsu* magazine. Also published in that year were Ueda Bin's *Uzumaki* (Vortex), Mushanokôji Saneatsu's *Omedetaki Hito* (The Good-Natured Man), Tanizaki Junichirô's *Shisei* (Tattoo) and *Zô* (An Elephant) and Yoshii Isamu's *Kawachiya Yohei*. The magazines, *Mita Bungaku, Shirakaba* and *The Second Shin Shichô* were also established.

Naturalism, on the other hand, was already past its peak and had lost its spark. But the writers of this school were still very productive, as indicated by *Ie* (Family) by Tôson, *Tsuchi* (Soil) by Nagatsuka Takashi, *Hôrô* (Wandering) by Hômei and *Bikô* (Faint Light) by Hakuchô.

This coexistence of aestheticism, the Shirakaba group (representing idealism) and naturalism during the late Meiji period was indicative of what the Taishô literary world would look like. The emergence some years later of such writers as Akutagawa Ryûnosuke, Kikuchi Kan and Satô Haruo only meant the addition of one more new school called Intellectualism to the existing literary currents.

If, for convenience's sake, we took the year 1910 as the beginning of the Shirakaba group and aestheticism, which later formed the foundation of Taishô literature, it would be interesting to see just how old the people who formed this new literary camp and the established naturalist writers they challenged were in this epoch-making year. For their ages will eloquently tell us about the nature of the literature of the day.

Nagai Kafû, who was regarded as the leader of the new literature and who even said that he was "the vanguard" of the age, was 31 years old, or just the same age as Masamune Hakuchô. Of the new writers of aestheticism who gathered around Kafû, Osanai Kaoru was 29; Tanizaki Junichirô and Yoshii Isamu, 24; Kinoshita Mokutarô, 25; Kubota Mantarô who was to win fame shortly with *Mita Bungaku* and *Subaru,* 21; Minakami Takitarô, 23; and Satô Haruo, 18.

In the Shirakaba group, Arishima Takeo at 32 was the oldest; Arishima

Ikuma, 28; Shiga Naoya, 27; Mushanokôji Saneatsu, 25; Satomi Ton and Nagayo Yoshio, 22.

When we consider the fact that even Ôgai and Sôseki, who were looked up to by young writers as elders, were only 50 and 44, respectively, the average age of the writers of this period was far younger than our common sense tells us is possible.

As for poets, Kitahara Hakushû who had issued *Jashûmon* (The Evil Faith) the year before, was 25, Ishikawa Takuboku who published *Ichiaku no Suna* (A Handful of Sand) was 24 and Takamura Kôtarô who returned from Paris that year was 27.

When we consider the weight these names carry in modern Japanese literary history, their youth is almost shocking. Even more amazing than the young age they started their careers with is that most of them had reached a sort of "maturity" within less than a decade.

Most of the Taishô writers began their activities in their twenties and had done most of their writing before they became 40. When we compare this with Meiji authors like Ôgai, Tôson and Katai, who had to lay a foundation patiently for their activities, and with the writers of today who, even in their 40's and 50's are still far from finding perfection of expression or peace of mind, it becomes clear that one unique feature of Taishô novels lies in this youthfulness.

It is true that the Taishô period was one of the richest periods in the history of the modern Japanese novel and that the greater part of the lasting masterpieces were turned out during this period. Most of these works, however, were mature products of the writers who, belonging to the pre-naturalism generation had been struggling along since the Meiji period. On the other hand, the representative writers of the new schools who were the main power to influence the literary world were, in many cases, young men who had grown up in a favorable environment. Their precocity which resulted from their easily finding a perfect expression in their youth, together with the disappearance of the hot-house-like social conditions in later years, forced many of them to end their writing careers while they were still young.

In no other age have young people had such a large voice in the
literature of the times and been feared more by the older generation,
while they themselves treated their elders with contempt and aloofness,
simply because they had been born later. They inherited this pride of
"newness" from naturalistic writers of the previous generation and
assimilated it more naturally than their forerunners. In this respect, they
were new.

However, as Satomi Ton has bitterly criticized himself later, while
young men still under 40, they as "great writers" had to stand up against
the challenges of the young Shôwa youths who attacked them using the
same weapon of "newness" making it more potent by attaching
"thought" to it.

The novels of the Taishô period seem, on the surface, to be varied and
complex. In essence, however, they are all expressions of the authors'
self-liberation in the hot house-like environment of the literary world.

As I mentioned before, the naturalistic movement in this country was,
in a sense, a romantic movement. It has both what Takuboku called the
"self-denying factor" and "self-asserting factor," the former being a
product of scientific rationalism and the latter coming from the desire
for self-liberation, the original mission of romanticism. The 'I' novel
was a form in which the two elements could easily be blended.

The history of the novel in the Taishô period was the history of the
development and the exhaustion of the 'I' novel. It was a process of the
'I' novel growing universal, purifying its contents and improving its
form until finally it was confronted with its inherent weak point.

Naturalism in Japan was not founded on a clear system of thought but
was rather the frank expression of the feelings toward life of the young
people of a certain period. Even young writers waving the flag of antinaturalism were breathing the same air as the naturalistic writers, as far
as the "mood" of their lives was concerned. Their literature was like
different stems branching out from the same root, be it aestheticism,
Shirakaba literature or naturalism.

Just as they were all mainly concerned with how to bring out and develop the selves that had been freed by the naturalists, they all adopted the 'I' novel or similar forms (even though the author does not take up his own life, he gives the impression that he is talking directly to the readers by founding the whole work on "realities").

The "human being" described by the naturalistic novelists was certainly liberated by the authors' denial of the established values and order. But at the same time, the very denial of existing values and order robbed the "human being" of the root of his desire for life.

The young writers who succeeded these naturalistic novelists, therefore, tried hard to colour in this almost inhuman, colourless spirit with individuality, thereby giving it a basis for positive living.

Basically, aestheticism, the Shirakaba group and the Intellectual shool that appeared later were all movements to give ethics to the novel. There were only subtle differences between them: among the aesthetics, ethics being coloured with a rebellious cultural taste against the conventional moral of society; while in the Shirakaba school, it took the form of enthusiastic self-righteous humanism.

CHAPTER XII

The Aesthetic School: Nagai Kafû and Tanizaki Jun'ichirô

Nagai Kafû is worth discussing not merely as an originator of the Aesthetic school, but as a great writer on a level with Ôgai and Sôseki for the wide scope of his works extending beyond the school of his followers and his long active literary life.

Born in Tokyo in 1879, Kafû's given name was Sôkichi. Though he had attracted some readers through his writings as a Zolaist in the 4th decade of Meiji (1897–1906), his original work is considered to start with *Amerika Monogatari* (The American Stories) and *Furansu Monogatari* (The French Stories), both the harvest of his early years (25–30) spent in America and France from 1903 to 1908. His writing, exotic for the Japanese and tinged with the melancholy of the Western world of those times, seemed to the young men of those days to be a new direction for literature to move away from the drabness of naturalism.

The ideas Kafû learned from his five-year stay abroad were deeper, however, than those found in these two youthfully sentimental books. In the harsh mercantile society of the United States, he learned about individual freedom and independence on which modern civilization was founded. In France, he realized how strongly traditions which the colonial life of the mechanized civilization of America seemed to lack, were alive in every phase of Western culture enriching it from inside. He returned home as critic burning with an intense dislike for the "false civilization" of the Meiji era. When it is seen with the ideals of civilization learned from these countries, Meiji culture appeared to him a superficial form constructed by the vanity of statesmen without regard to the true happiness of the people.

Kafû's critical zeal for civilization was boldly expressed in most of his works written soon after returning home, mainly in 1909: *Kitsune* (The Fox), *Shinkichôsha Nikki* (A Diary of a Person Recently Returned from Abroad), *Kanraku* (Pleasure), *Fukagawa no Uta* (A Song of Fukagawa), *Kangokusho no Ura* (In Back of the Prison), *Shukuhai* (A Toast), *Botan no Kyaku* (The Peony Garden), and *Reishô* (Sneers). Of these, *Shinkichôsha Nikki, Kangokusho no Ura* and *Reishô* especially show the author's thought most concretely.

Kafû's criticism of Meiji culture was homogeneous to that of Ôgai, Sôseki, or Futabatei. A passionate indignation or sarcasm was directed against the obstinate people, who were subjected to the pressures of Western civilization introduced in the form of what Sôseki termed the "externally induced enlightenment," for their fascination with external successes that caused them to lose harmony in their inner lives.

As a matter of course, any Japanese visiting Europe in the Meiji era must have been aware of the inferiority of Japan attempting to imitate Western civilization superficially and not even attaining that. Kafû's criticisms had much in common with the extravagant impressions of most "persons recently returned from abroad." They would keep these impressions in mind for a while, but soon forget them as they again became accustomed to Japanese life. Takuboku correctly commented that Kafû's criticism had some disagreeableness comparable to that of a young rustic finding fault with the costume of country geishas after he had been on a spree with geishas in the city.

Kafû was original, however, in devoting his life to keeping this attitude of a "person recently returned from abroad," making it the true basis for his work. This attitude influenced his thinking all his life, and was further strengthened as a basis for his inner life by becoming a part of his ex-pressed thought. He, perhaps as well as Ôgai and Sôseki, knew the significance of traditions in European civilization causing him to idealize the Japan of the past; it was more than a mere retrospective taste for the past, it was a passionate and ethical zeal for the Japanese civilization of the past that had fallen victim to the "new civilization" transplanted into this country in the Meiji era. While in Ôgai this passionate zeal worked for reproducing the past based on scientific truth and in Sôseki acted in making the past a background for contrast with his contemporary time clearly showing the absence of ethics for his day, in Kafû, more than ten years younger than both of them, it grew to be an enthusiastic admiration of old relics and customs of the Edo period still remaining in downtown Tokyo, and was further crystallized into an almost eccentric adoration of the gay quarters which still preserved much of the customs of those days when happiness could be built on "ignorance and superstition."

The writings of Kafû and his followers were called aesthetic and were denounced as debauched literature, exciting the curiosity of the public. Among those who gathered around him and looked upon him as their leader were Tanizaki Junichirô, Yoshii Isamu, Nagata Mikihiko and Osanai Kaoru. With the remnants of feudalistic morality regarding the pleasures of life as vicious still rampant, it must have been significant enough that they depicted the world of dissipation without scruple in their works. In the days when even naturalistic writers could not allow themselves the pleasures of love except as a means of "self-culture," Kafû and his followers openly extolled the beauty of the female flesh and declared love or the "pleasures of the senses" the goal of life. As far as frankness was concerned, they are a step more advanced than their contemporaries. It was for this reason that Kafû's works were respected as a theoretical or artistic pattern by writers of that period. Until the background of this period is understood, Tanizaki Junichirô's remark: "The most substantial influence we have received from Western literature is the liberation of love," cannot be fully perceived.

Even to those with the most liberal minds, emancipation was strictly for men. Among the freedoms achieved, however, was the freedom to kneel to women, enabling the writers belonging to this school to create women as embodiments of beauty and evil, such as never existed in the Japanese novel before. Tanizaki Junichirô spent over half of his lifetime in such creations.

The Aesthetic school, in a sense, was a revival of urban tastes, a rebirth of curiousity toward the colourful, unknown and abnormal, against the naturalistic literature, flat and prosaic descriptions of everyday life, by writers of provincial birth. The school had a connection to the past common to that of the "licensed quarters" literature by the members of Kenyûsha. Although it strongly appealed to the rebellious instinct of the young men, its theoretical base was not firm enough to sustain interest over a long period. Gradually, the Shirakaba school in 1929–30 took the Aesthetic school's position as the center of ideas for those times, after the Aesthetic school's few years of prosperity following Naturalism. Takamura Kôtarô's career was typical of this trend: after returning from Paris in 1910, he joined the anti-naturalistic movement of the Pan no Kai (Pan Society) and Humanitarianism which indicates the development of his ingenuity.

Nevertheless, many of the members of the Aesthetic school, as they had been born and brought up in the metropolis inclining them to be more individualistic, continued on their respective ways producing excellent works even after the influence of their school had declined. Tanizaki Junichirô is typical of such hardworking individualists. Nagai Kafû also pursued his own unique course of maturity.

Kafû's preference for the gay quarters was essentially born from a rebellious spirit with a martyr-like pride in getting himself involved enough in the atmosphere of the gay quarters without giving himself up to it. When Kafû's works are compared with Chikamatsu Shûkô's *Kurokami* (Dark Hair), it is quite evident that this rugged philanderer was never ensnared in love. To him, the licensed quarters were a "paradise for exiles" which gave intellectual rather than emotional satisfaction. Getting acquainted with this world of "shame and vice" was to learn about the other side of the polite society of the Meiji era that he so abhorred. In all of his writings about the gay quarters, unlike the works of his juniors, there is not even the slightest intoxication with the sentiment of this particular world. A certain dry intellect is even noticeable in the rich style of his early masterpieces. Though this characteristic might be detrimental to a novelist and was a consequence of his attitude to the world, it did give him a literary life much longer than the school in which he had begun.

As the cultural critic in him gradually transformed this individualistic way of thinking about the gay quarters into an extremely popularized form, the author of the clumsy intellectual novel, *Reishô* (Sneers), after making such an unusual detour, became a refined social novelist, a historian of manners and customs.

In the novel, *Udekurabe* (Rivalry) written in 1916, the manners of the red-light district at Shimbashi and the morals of the gentlemen who patronized it are depicted methodically through the heroine, Komayo. Though the characters somewhat lack individuality, it is truly a novel of manners, a rarity in the Taishô era. *Udekurabe,* however, was the last of his works depicting the manners and customs of the gay quarters in this way. As the traditions of the past gradually went to ruin in the gay world itself, the themes of his novels moved to cafés, unlicensed prostitutes, and dance-hall girls that represented the new urban manners. Though outwardly taking the form of women of the new age, his heroines in these works were more and more vividly depicted as women of such old-fashioned and good character as to be, in essence, a reversal in his ideal woman. The heroine, waitress Kimie, of *Tsuyu no Atosaki* (During the Rains, 1931), and the heroines, unlicensed prostitutes, of *Hikage no Hana* (Flowers in the Shade, 1934) and *Bokutô Kidan* (Romance from the East of the Sumida River, 1937) were all living in the abyss of modern urban manners, and yet had at the bottom of their ignorant souls, the goodness of the common people. These women feeling ashamed of their own plight and despised by the public were not conscious of their pureness of heart; in this very point Kafû found the materials about which he could write with the greatest sympathy in his times. His success as a novelist is in his gradually making the ethical character of his heroines more and more distinct in proportion as the traditional gay world was dying. Along with this, his style moved from the somewhat affected lyrical touch of the early period to the plain and dry one of the works coming after *Tsuyu no Atosaki.*

It is characteristic of Western modern literature that the writers of what we call the Aesthetic school were severe cultural critics or moralists at the core while outwardly the immoral lives they lived were the practise of their own criticisms. Kafû was rather exceptional in this country for possessing a theoretical criterion common to those of the aesthetic novelists of the West, though a little inclined to ethics as he was an Oriental. Kafû's distinguishing trait was that on the soil of contemporary Japanese literature, which could not nurture the Romantic school except in a mutated form, he was able to mature to an unusually large degree as a romantic poet. This was due to the favourable environment of his youth and his strong will power. Kafû is worthy of the attention of many literary historians as a living example of the deepest influence that European literature, with French literature as its center, produced on Japanese writers. If some form of estrangement from the climate and customs of one's native land should be a basic element of romantic literature, exile and flight being its starting point, and if the other side of this sentiment should be the yearning for some country on earth as the promised land, then America and France were the realization of this for Kafû. Symbolically, they were the breasts which nurtured the infancy of this romantic poet, born in the sea-girt little kingdom of the Far East, into a full-fledged adult. Once he wrote, "I wish I had been born in a country where I could cry to my heart's content if I were hit on the head than in this country where people are supposed to be as strong as the redoubtable hero Benkei and bear everything in silence." His experience of actually living in these two countries in his youthful days satisfied this desire to some extent teaching him what modern life and literature were like and correspondingly what shapes they were taking in the "country where the people are as stoic as Benkei."

A true romanticist, he did not wish to fill the gap developed between him and his native country. On the contrary, he found sincerity and glory as a poet in a lifelong solitude compensating for this gap. The reader may consider him as either having been faithful to his own ideas established in his youth throughout the long span of his literary life, or as having learned nothing from Japanese society from the time he returned from abroad remaining enslaved by a childish impression causing him to face everything in his native land with a strange preconception. In either case, however, anyone who reads his essays written in his later years cannot deny that to Kafû this way of thinking became habitual, affecting all he wrote. All harlots from his pen, from Komayo of *Udekurabe* to Chiyomi of *Odoriko* (Dancing Girl), were characters on whom he rested his dreams for existence in this solitary life; they were human patterns molded in the same fashion as the heroines of all modern novels from Chateaubriand to Gide.

In the last part of the Meiji period, after disassociating himself from the literary movements, Kafû reminisced that he was in those days "beating, a war drum in the avant-garde of the literary world." Tanizaki Jun'ichirô, one of the new writers coming to the call of this drum, was a most brilliant figure. He was born in Tokyo in 1886 and studied literature at Tokyo University, leaving it without taking a degree. From early in his life Tanizaki admired Kafû as his model, considering him a literary blood-relative. In 1910, he brought out the magazine *Shin Shichô* (New Currents of Thought), the second magazine under that name, with Watsuji Tetsurô, Kimura Sôhachi, and others under the leadership of Osanai Kaoru. *Shisei* (Tattoo), *Kirin* (Prodigy) and other short stories were published in this magazine. In the following year, 1911, he wrote *Shônen* (A Boy) and *Hôkan* (The Jester) for the magazine *Subaru* (Pleiades). These works won recognition from such literary men as Ôgai and Ueda Bin. His fame as a novelist, however, was suddenly but firmly established after Nagai Kafû offered his highest tribute by publishing an essay entitled "Tanizaki Junichirô's Works" in the November issue of the *Mita Bungaku*, 1911. In it Kafû wrote, "The one who has succeeded in opening up a phase of art which no one at all in the modern literary world of the Meiji era has been able to, or has dared to set his hand to, is Jun'ichirô Tanizaki." Thus, he had the good fortune to win recognition through the laudatory essay by Nagai Kafû, whom he admired from youth. After that, he continued to grow favourably as a novelist publishing one after another of his fine works, including *Akuma* (Demon) in 1912, *Zoku Akuma* (Second Demon) and *Koi o Shiru Koro* (Adolescence) in 1913, and *Haru no Umibe* (The Beach in Spring) and *Jôtarô* in 1914. Tanizaki came to attain a reputation toward the end of the Taishô era surpassing that of Kafû.

The characteristic feature of Tanizaki's art is his non-resistance to beauty and vice originating from his thoroughly sensual peculiarity to possess women by being conquered by them rather than by conquering them, while Kafû's attitude toward pleasures was grounded on what might be called the ethics within beauty and vice. In Kafû's *demi-monde* literature, women are treated as a tool for men's pleasures, while in Jun'ichirô's works, men are only "manure" for nurturing the beauty of women, as declared in his maiden work, *Shisei*. In this respect, Jun'ichirô was a step more aesthetic than Kafû. In the early part of his literary career, in particular, he was ardent to become a martyr to beauty by writing about all sorts of vice that female beauty could bring on males. In this period, he shocked the public by writing without the least hesitation about such sexual abnormalities as masochism and fetishism. His detailed description of the young man in *Akuma* licking the soiled handkerchief of his sweetheart became renowned as the epitome of aestheticism.

As the leadership shifted from Kafû to Junichirô, Japanese aestheticism lost the theoretical criterion of cultural criticism, and at the same time got rid of androcentric egoism. Its course tended toward men's placing women at the center of the world and discovering their happiness in an ecstasy of the senses by obediently submitting and kneeling to their charms. This was the difference in the traits of the late Meiji era and the Taishô era. It was also the starting point for the literature of a new age to begin perfecting itself.

The years 1910 and 1911, when Kafû was inclined to be silent and Junichirô made his gallant appearance, were those of the Kôtoku Shûsui high-treason affair. In a passage from his well-known novel, *Hanabi* (Fireworks), Kafû writes, "In 1911, when I was teaching at Keiô University, I more than once witnessed on my way there five or six prison vans running along Ichigaya Street in the direction to the court-house at Hibiya. Never before in my life have I experienced an event that gave me such a feeling of disgust. As a man of letters, I ought not to have remained silent, but I kept silent as other literary men did. Some-how, I felt I was not able to bear the pain of my conscience. I felt extremely ashamed of being a man of literature. Ever since I have felt it best to abase my own art to the same degree that the *gesaku* writer of the Edo period did." It is difficult to know how seriously he took this, but it is certain, at any rate, that he was deeply affected by the unsparing suppression of thought starting with the Kôtoku affair, making him painfully conscious that his own theoretical criterion was too feeble to repel this pressure.

On the other hand, to Junichirô who did not have such a criterion from the beginning, the Kôtoku affair was nothing more than a mere outside event unrelated to his inner life as an artist. He may have felt repugnance for the atmosphere of oppression that followed the event, but it was unthinkable for him to "feel ashamed of being a man of literature." This was his strength as a literary man of the rising generation. While Kafû was beginning to wear a tobacco-pouch at his side, collect Ukiyoe, and play the samisen, Junichirô avidly studied Western writers of the aesthetic school or the art-for-art's-sake school of Wilde, Baudelaire and Anatole France and energetically continued to produce literature in his florid style in praise of woman and sexual aberrations leading from her beauty. *Osai to Minosuke* (Osai and Minosuke, 1915) and *Fumiko no Ashi* (The Legs of Fumiko, 1919) are representative of these works.

These sensual hymns he sang in praise of feminine beauty represent one phase of the spirit of the times and served to break down the remaining feudalistic customs, just as the entire movement of the Aesthetic school did, but since the hymns after all were only possible when males were assumed to be extreme idiots, the limitations to human liberation in his works were soon obvious. Gradually maturing as a writer, he took notice of this and came to write his tragedies with males captivated by feminine beauty as the main characters. *Chijin no Ai* (A Fool's Love), the first novel he wrote after moving from Tokyo to the Kansai district because of the great earthquake-fire of 1923, was a masterpiece in creating such a hero for the first time. Later on, his unique ethics that man's true happiness consisted in being conquered by women found its highest expression in *Shunkinshô* (The Story of Shunkin, 1919). Living in Kansai, he made new discoveries in the traditional beauty of old Japan. *Tade kuu Mushi* (Some Prefer Nettles, 1929) is a masterpiece dealing with a middle-aged couple's crisis, something he was experiencing at the time, effectively interlaced with his sentiments on his discoveries from his own experience. During and after the Second World War, he wrote *Sasame-yuki* (The Makioka Sisters) exhaustively depicting the modern manners and customs of Kansai in this monumental work on the inner life of a family. This long work is said to have been based on Junichirô's new relatives from his third marriage. In this novel, the male character, considered to be another self of the author, proves that an exact counterpart of Sasuke, the hero of *Shunkinshô,* can live in the form of a fine modern gentleman. Even in his historical novels, *Mômoku Monogatari* (The Story of the Blind One, 1931) and *Shôshô Shigemoto no Haha* (The Mother of Court-Noble Shigemoto, 1949), his worship of the female is clearly evident.

CHAPTER XIII

Mori Ôgai

Mori Ôgai and Ueda Bin cooperated in editing the magazine, *Subaru* (Pleiades), and occupied positions of elders in the movement of the Aesthetic school. Ueda Bin's *Kaichô On* (The Sound of the Tide), a collection of European poems superbly rendered into Japanese and published in 1905, marked a new epoch in the history of modern poetry in this country. It was held in high esteem both as a competent introduction of the new trends in foreign literature and as a capable criticism of naturalism. Ueda went abroad for study in 1907 and soon after returning home was appointed professor at Kyôto University. After that he remained outside the literary world of the metropolis except for a long novel, *Uzumaki* (Vortex), a semi-autobiography representing a refined Epicurianism written in 1910 for *Kokumin Shimbun* making a deep impression on the young men.

Compared with this, Ôgai's activity was much more versatile and significant. The several years which succeeded the first publication of *Subaru* in 1909 might be called the period of his second youth as a literary man; his creative power revived at that time did not lose its vigor until he died in November 1922. These productive ten-odd years may be roughly divided into three periods by the nature of his works.

The first period begins in 1909 with the publishing of *Hannichi* (Half a Day), *Kamen* (Mask), *Ita Sekusuarisu* (Vita Sexualis) and others in quick succession in the *Subaru* and ends in the last year of Meiji (1911). Most of his modern-life novels including *Gan* (The Wild Goose, 1911), *Seinen* (Young Man, 1910) and *Môsô* (Illusion, 1911) were written in this period.

In the second period, he wrote *Okitsu Yagoemon no Isho* (The Suicide

Note of Okitsu Yagoemon, October 1912) strongly influenced by the self-immolation of General Nogi on the death of Emperor Meiji. In this period, he published other historical novels and short stories such as *Abe Ichizoku* (The Abe Clan, 1913), *Ôshio Heihachirô* (1914), *Sanshôdayû* (1915) and *Takase Bune* (The Boat on the Takase River, 1916).

In the third period, becoming dissatisfied with fiction dealing with imaginary characters and events, he began to write historical biographies and research. *Shibue Chûsai, Izawa Ranken* and *Hôjô Katei* are representative of this period.

Ôgai was already near fifty years of age when *Subaru* was started, making him rather hesitant to join the new literary movement of young people in his declining years, but as the new literature of the day, including naturalism, could in a sense be interpreted as the fruit of his long effort for enlightenment from the days of the magazine *Shigarami Zôshi*, it stimulated him into further activity, especially when he saw his own efforts of half a lifetime ripening into a shape quite unsatisfactory.

This feeling is traceable in the starting part of *Ita Sekusuarisu*. In those days, it was characteristic for him to face anything and everything with a critical attitude. He did not alter this attitude of questioning coldly, "What for?" toward his own motives for writing as well as toward matters of the world and naturalism. In *Ita Sekusuarisu*, he writes that he was doing such unusual things as confessing only because he intended it to be of some use as reference data for his son. When this attitude, "What for?" was pushed to the extreme, he finally came to consider office work and art on the same level, neither worthy of any serious attention. He writes in *Asobi* (Play), "At any rate, anything Kimura (Everyman) does is play to him. So if he should play at all, it will be better for him to play with what he likes and finds interesting than with what he does not. But no matter how interesting, if he continues to do it all the time, he will find it monotonous and soon be bored with it." This sagacious sceptic gave the impression of trying to regard art lightly lest his creative capacity gradually decrease as his taste grew more and more fastidious with age. Ôgai wrote in *Môsô,* "I have met many a teacher but not a single master. And I have learned that metaphysics, however exquisitely constructed, is no better than a lyric poem" Ôgai was a modern with the surest background of natural science among all the literati throughout the Meiji and Taishô periods, preferring to spend his later years with only a Zeiss microscope and Merz telescope as his companions. Even from the time he was in his twenties, Ôgai found the value and authority of all traditions denied by this new weapon of the human spirit, natural science, and felt a "keen sense of emptiness in mind." On such occassions, he looked again into every fact with the reasoning of natural science, but found little consolation. This seems to be the main reason for his gradually giving up novels for his final work, historical biographies. At any rate, this epicurean had more interest in analyzing pleasures than in pleasures themselves; even his "play" in-cluded art.What he learned from naturalism was only the reckless power of execution that his juniors had acquired from their half-boiled theories. He sketched self-potraits in various forms in their manner. The distinc-tive feature of these works in his *Subaru* days is that the heroes describing the ways of life they observe and the author who describes them are coldly depicted as if they had no relation to Ôgai. If it is the attitude of a natural scientist to observe the objects of his study as they are and describe them as such without a particle of emotion, then there are few novels more naturally scientific than those of Ôgai.

Although the characters of the heroes all have some resemblance to the author, they are lightly caricatured. This intentional rendering of the characters commonplace is not only sometimes disagreeable, but it lowers the whole tone of his works giving the impression that he is still immature as a novelist. Perhaps, it is not a mere accident that, of his works written in this period, *Gan* and *Seinen* which amply reflect his personal experiences with their intricate windings, generally excel both in quality and quantity. Ôgai seems unconsciously to be greatly discon-tented with his own inability to write his novels rather than with the passiveness of his characters. In short, this first period is to be considered a preparatory one for Ôgai, for his real genius in his later years was given full play in the sphere of historical novels and biographies.

The Kôtoku affair of June 1910 was a shock to him. The ensuing almost insane pressure of the authorities on speech and writing especially led him to write *Chimmoku no Tô* (Silent Tower) and *Shokudô* (Dining Hall). The attitude of these times that would not permit the separation of legend and history in thinking about the "fundamental character of the country" induced him also to write *Kanoyôni* (As If). However, as he had always been a conservative, this affair did not cause him more than surprise that anarchism and socialism, merely objects of his intellectual interest, had actually resulted in creating such an incident in this country, and worry about the childishness of the policy the government had adopted toward it. It was, after all, only an external influence.

General Nogi's self-immolation occuring two years later, however, greatly shocked him, motivating him to write the historical work, *Okitsu Yagoemon no Isho* soon after he heard the news of General Nogi's suicide. This short story reveals the principles which amount to the theme of all his historical writings: "From the viewpoint of the utilitarian, all good things in this world would cease to exist," or, "If tea ceremonies were empty forms, the august ceremonials of the state together with ancestor-worship rituals would be empty forms also." In this novel, there is an admiration or envy of the life of the samurai who lived only for the sake of honor, free of utilitarianism, dying a peaceful death.

Ôgai was a rationalist, but having been influenced by the "learning" of the German Empire at its height, it was easy for him from his own experience to understand how the transplantation of Western civilization exclusively done on the basis of utilization had caused Japan of his day to develop into a notorious utilitarian nation.

While he endured this "emptiness of mind," he felt strongly dissatisfied with the deluge of insincere utilitarians who were not even conscious of this emptiness. In this phenomenon, he found an extreme uncertainty in the future of Japan. This may explain why he was particularly stirred by how the Japanese people lived according to a different mode of morality a hundred years before. Thus, writing historical works was for him an attempt at cultural criticism.

Ôgai, like Kafû and Sôseki, was a critic who had constantly on his mind the problems of the character and the fate of the contemporary culture of this country. Unlike Sôseki, however, he did not try to solve these problems by depicting his contemporaries, but sought in the old pages of history some characters near his ideals and recreated their lives. It may be that he attempted to fathom the secret of the peculiar psychology of the Japanese and tried to search for possiblities in the Japanese spirit beyond the prevailing utilitarianism in doing so.

His historical novels have no retrospective or dilettantish element at all in their motifs. His spirit was eagerly trying to find a guiding principle in life, just like the personages in his works lying between life and death. When he was writing that there had really existed such a person with an ideal life and who died such a death, he was really criticizing the people of his own age. This belief in the past gave him hope for the living. This is the reason why *Abe Ichizoku, Jîsan Bâsan* (An Old Couple), and *Takase Bune* leave profound Greek-tragedy-like impressions on the reader about the meaning of destiny, life and death of the human being. Naturally, this attitude could not but cause the center of his interest to shift from novels to historical biographies and investigations in which "the past is described as it was" by "carefully studying historical materials and making it a principle to respect the 'nature' discovered in them." *Kuriyama Daizen* and *Sugihara Shina,* both written in 1915, are short works in which he follows these principles of consciously avoiding novel-like colouring. After publishing the masterpiece, *Shibue Chûsai* in 1916, he untiringly continued to write a large number of historical biographies until he died.

Of all his historical works, he spent his greatest efforts on the lives of Confucian scholars in the Tokugawa period like Shibue Chûsai, Izawa Ranken and Hôjô Katei whose method of study was to explain the Chinese classics without dogma based on the evidence found in historical documents. These scholars neither made any scholastic achievements to largely benefit posterity nor did they establish enduring literary fame. If Ôgai had failed to excavate them by mere chance, they would have still been buried in oblivion. In their commonplace appearance and monotonous lives, Ôgai recognized their passionate ardor for learning and noble way of living, truly worthy of the name of man, indifferent to worldly success and contented with their lot.

Partly because these biographies of scholars appeared serially in daily newspapers, they were not taken seriously, even by many of his intimate acquaintances. To this kind of attitude, Ôgai writes at one place, "I do not like to discuss as to whether my writing of these biographies is useful or not. I write them only because I wish to," and in another place, "There is no difference in the meaning between the writing of the life of a hero like Bismarck and the writing of the life of a crippled Confucianist like Ranken in the service of the Abe family." These words brimming with self-confidence are evidence that Ôgai found the ideal for the Japanese in such Confucian scholars and that he was hopeful that their very existence in the past could arouse inspiration in the minds of the people for the future of the country. He writes at the beginning of *Shibue Chûsai*, "Chûsai is a man who walked the same path as I do. But he did it far better. He had much stronger legs to walk on. He is to me an awe-inspiring person." This shows plainly and aptly how he looked up to the heroes of these historical biographies.

In April 1916, Ôgai resigned from his post of surgeon in the Army where he had served for many years. In December 1917, he was appointed Curator of the Imperial Museum and Chief Librarian. He started writing *Teishi Kô* (A Study on Imperial Posthumous Names) in August 1919 and published it from the Department of the Imperial Household in 1921. Then he proceeded to write *Gengô Kô* (A Study on Reign Names) but he passed away in July 1922 at sixty years of age without finishing it. Atrophy of the kidney was the disease according to his doctor, but some say it was pulmonary tuberculosis.

CHAPTER XIV

Natsume Sôseki

Natsume Sôseki stood aloof from the main stream of the literary circles of the day to the same extent that Ôgai did, and was respected as another star of the first magnitude. However, just as Ôgai was rather close to the Aesthetic school through his activities for *Subaru* and *Mita Bungaku*, so was Sôseki close to and so respected by the young men of the Shirakaba school that the literary section of the *Asahi Shimbun* over which he had control became a flowery arena for testing the talents of many rising writers including those belonging to that school.

Natsume Sôseki (real name, Kinnosuke) was born in Tokyo in 1867. Graduating from Tokyo University in 1890, he spent the first half of his life as an English teacher at Matsuyama and Kumamoto. Then after studying in England from 1900 to 1903, he became a professor at the First High School and concurrently a lecturer at Tokyo University.

From his student days at the First High School he had regularly composed *haiku* (seventeen-syllabled verses) with the encouragement of Masaoka Shiki, his close friend. When he published his maiden novel, *Wagahai wa Neko de Aru* (I am a Cat) in *Hototogisu* (Cuckoo), a haiku magazine by invitation of its editor, Takahama Kyoshi in 1905, his fame was suddenly established. Next, he wrote *Botchan* (My Dear Little Master), *Rondon Tô* (The Tower of London) and *Kusamakura* (The Grass Pillow) dazzling the reading public with his extraordinary and abundant literary talent. In 1907, he resigned from all his posts in the teaching profession and joined the *Asahi Shimbun,* for which he first wrote *Gubijinsô* (The Red Poppy). This was followed by *Kôfu* (the Mine-Worker, 1908), *Sanshirô* (1908), *Sorekara* (And Then, 1909), *Mon* (The Gate, 1910), *Higansugi Made* (Till after the Spring Equinox, 1912), *Kôjin* (Passers-by,

1913), *Kokoro* (The Mind, 1914), *Michikusa* (Loitering, 1915) and the unfinished work, *Meian* (Light and Shade, 1916). He published novel after novel of high order in this way, serially, in the *Asahi Shimbun* every year except for a period of about one year and a half between *Mon* and *Higansugi Made* when he had to take a rest on account of a severe stomach ulcer. This abnormally high rate of production is not only indicative of his superabundant literary talent, but also of a frantic effort on his part. The works in his early period, written when he was still an "amateur" such as *Wagahai wa Neko de Aru* and *Botchan* suggest the spontaneous combustion of long-suppressed talent in their writing and exhibit the outflow of great genius rarely found in the modern literary history of this country. *Gubijinsô* and the other long novels which followed it, written after he had made a name for himself as a professional writer, clearly indicate that keeping production at this rate is more than ordinary health can possibly bear; these were without exception written from thoroughly studied framework in a style polished and repolished to the last degree.

His works from *Higansugi Made* up to his death have especially the sparks of a gallant spirit of a man who ruins his already failing health further by novel writing and is still eager to devote the remaining span of his life to it. Like many other great novelists, Sôseki had what might be called the problems of life and death challenging his spirit. He was so intent on expressing these problems that his own life was not important. Whether he could live a few years longer or not was nothing to him in this state of mind. Then what were the problems that he so eagerly pursued and wanted to make clear even at the cost of his life? They were firstly the character of Japanese contemporary culture which he deeply mistrusted, and secondly "egoism" of modern people which was inseparable from the first problem.

Even when he graduated with a high reputation from the English Literature department of the university, he had had doubts about the very meaning of learning English literature in Japan. Then, he further had still graver doubts about the methods and the results of the Japanese introducing Western civilization into its culture; he found himself constantly agonized by an "inward restlessness about his swaggering about in a borrowed mantle." This uneasiness or irritation reached its height during his stay in London causing some of his acquaintances to think he had gone mad. Briefly, his unrest originated from his having no grounds for supporting his own opinion in the judgement of a literary work if his opinion should differ from that of an Englishman, as he did not have much confidence in his ability to appreciate the English language on a par with him. In order to dispel this unrest, therefore, he made up his mind while staying in London to concentrate all of his energies on the study of literature by a scientific and positive method, and in accordance with the standards established through this study, to "build a new standpoint of his own" avoiding the necessity of using only his taste in judging literature. As a result of such a minute scientific study, of which a glimpse is given in his *Bungaku Ron* (Essays on Literature) published later, he confessed that now he had decided on an "autonomous" position and discovered the course he should take, he had become "able to look at gloomy London with a light heart." On the other hand, his doubts about the character of the contemporary Japanese culture formed by the importation of Western culture grew more and more serious while staying in England. Even after he returned home these doubts continued to keep him rumored to be a "neurasthenic and lunatic," but at the same time, these same doubts came to constitute the nucleus of his novels.

According to Sôseki, the characteristic of Meiji civilization was: Japan had made an unreasonable and imprudent attempt to absorb foreign civilization like a "frog that tries to swallow a bull" and "had fallen into a more miserable condition because she had rashly expanded her range of contacts with the West." The root of all this calamity was that her entire culture was "compelled to achieve an unnatural development against her own will" by an external force. As a result of her desperate endeavour to catch up in a short period with the civilization which other races, superior both in brains and physique, had spent a great many years to build, Japan could not undertake her transition methodically: "since she could not afford the time to take one after another all the necessary steps of enlightenment, she walked them away so fast with the biggest possible strides that her feet could hardly touch more than a foot of the earth in covering ten feet of it, the remaining nine feet being as good as not walked on at all." Again, touching on the question, "What psychological effects does such external enlightenment exert on us?" he concludes, "a people who undergo such enlightenment must have a sense of emptiness and correspondingly feelings of discontent and un-easiness in some way.

Such an observation is principally much the same as those from the days of Futabatei made by several of the clear-sighted men of letters on the character of our modern civilization. In the later period, Ôgai and Kafû say in effect the same thing. Sôseki's originality, however, lies in his clearly grasping this emptiness in the spiritual life of the people caused by the external pressures of Western civilization, as an ethical problem for the intelligentsia who represented the people. This was to be the central theme in all his works. For Sôseki, this cultural pressure has its influence exclusively on the inner life of human beings and its immediate effects are on the intellectuals. To those who have no needs of an inner life (whether they may be noblemen, wealthy men, or the so-called commoners) civilization exists only at the outside of their lives, and therefore the introduction of Western civilization is no problem as long as it brings them material benefits, such as new ornaments for their lives, means of acquiring wealth, or improvements in sanitation.

From the position of the intelligentsia who ought to be the producers of culture as compared to these consumers of it, the matter is quite dif-ferent. If they possess a conscience deserving their social standing and mission, and if, in their pursuit of learning or when subjected to other influence in the spheres of art and literature, "they try to accomplish what others have acquired through a hundred years toil in ten years in a thorough-going manner, they must have stamina ten times as strong since the length of period allotted to them is only one tenth." If they were to run such a hopeless race in real earnest with "Westerners superior in both brains and physique," they would be sure to have a nervous break-down or fall sick. Consequently, it has become a common practice for them to shirk their tasks; such intellectual insincerity necessarily results in moral unfaithfulness. Therefore, the intelligentsia "who are inflated with pride like a peacock showing its feathers" cannot justify their existence since the ethics which formed the backbone of their scholarly attainments have collapsed and gone. Sôseki means this when he writes, "They must have a sense of emptiness in some way."

Western civilization has influenced the Japanese in such a way that it has given the general run of the people a sense of equality only in form while causing their desires to expand indefinitely. At the same time, it has reduced the intelligentsia to what might be called slavery to the "ego" which causes the loss of their inner ethical standards, with the result that the consciousness of liberty and equality they have obtained through contact with foreign civilization only serves to detach them from real happiness. Sôseki considered that here lay the biggest question of modern civilization. He took an interest in the mode of life of intellectuals as the direct manifestation of this problem. Thus, all his novels from *Wagahai wa Neko de Aru* to *Meian* consistently deal with educated men as their principal characters.

Naturally, destructive influences of modern thought were phenomena also noticeable in Europe, and Japan introduced such influences too. Gerhart Hauptmann's *Einsame Menschen* (Lonely Men) gained the sympathy of part of the Japanese literary and intellectual worlds and gave some hints to Katai for his *Futon* (The Quilt) , but Sôseki was original in firmly grasping and ceaselessly pursuing a clarification of how this same problem was taking a unique shape in the life and consciousness of ordinary intellectuals, apart from the particular society of letters, still more severely than in Europe. The problem was a combination of an "externally induced" civilization with the lack of sufficient economic power to sustain it. Sôseki, however, who advocated, "Follow heaven and eliminate ego" in his remaining years, does not seem to have ever solved this problem. It remains as one of the fundamental questions even today that society cannot work out; here is the basic reason why works of Sôseki, who died in 1916, have continued to be read until today so widely and not necessarily for what we call pure literature.

A man of rich educational temperament, Sôseki had an outstanding following. Besides Terada Torahiko who had constantly looked up to him as his teacher since the Fifth High School days, there were Abe Jirô, Abe Yoshishige, Komiya Toyotaka, Suzuki Miekichi, Nogami Toyo-ichirô and his wife Yaeko, Morita Sôhei, Akutagawa Ryûnosuke and Kume Masao among those who had master-pupil relations with him, though each with some difference in degree of depth and intimacy.

Suzuki Miekichi, who had been strongly influenced by the prose sketches of the Hototogisu school, rose in literary fame through his *Chidori* (The Plover, 1906) and *Yamabiko* (Echo, 1907). He was for a time also under the influence of naturalism and wrote *Kotori no Su* (The Nest of the Little Birds, 1910) and others. By writing to create a romantic world of his own with his delicate sense and urbane lyricism, he regained his true individuality through the excellent work, *Kuwa no Mi* (The Mulberries, 1914). In his later years, he spent much effort on juvenile literature. Editing the magazine, *Akai Tori* (The Red Bird) for many years, he endeavoured to create juvenile stories having literary value.

Not a disciple of Sôseki, but another man who changed from a novelist to a writer of juvenile stories about that time and achieved great things was Ogawa Mimei. He had a romantic character bearing some resemblance to that of Miekichi. Although a graduate of Waseda University, he was not a part of the naturalist movement. He published *Akai Fune* (The Red Boat), his first collection of juvenile stories in 1910 and *Rodon na Neko* (The Slow-Witted Cat), a novel of medium length, rather autobiographical, in 1912. Later on, he became a socialist joining the movement in its incipient stage. As his ideas had anarchistic tendencies, however, he was soon isolated from the current of the times and finally devoted himself to writing children's stories. He wrote nearly a thousand remarkable juvenile stories based on romanticism and humanitarianism.

Morita Sôhei started his literary activity deeply influenced by Continental literature. In his *Baien* (Black Smoke, 1909), a long novel that brought him fame, he depicted the love and attempted double suicide of a man obsessed with fin-de-siècle ideas and a highly egotistic lady.

This was based on his own love affair after the manner of Gabriele D'Annunzio's *Il Trionfo della Morte* (The Triumph of Death). This work was very popular mainly because the public knew that the characters came from life. Another autobiographical novel, *Rinne* (The Transmigration of Souls) and a retrospective criticism on Sôseki both written in 1923 are some other representative works of Morita.

Besides those mentioned above, Nagatsuka Takashi, a *waka* (thirty-one-syllabled verse) poet wrote *Tsuchi* (Soil, 1910) for the *Asahi Shimbun* through Sôseki's recommendation; Takahama Kyoshi, a *haiku* poet and a friend of Sôseki, wrote *Kaki Futatsu* (Two Persimmons, 1915), a long prose sketch of his teacher, Shiki; and Itô Sachio, another *Waka* poet who published the pathetic story, *Nogiku no Haka* (The Grave with Wild Chrysanthemum, 1906) in *Hototogisu* at about the same time as Sôseki's *Wagahai wa Neko de Aru* was published; are all to be remembered as novelists for the single work each did, mentioned above.

CHAPTER XXV

The Shirakaba School: Mushanokôji, Shiga and Others

The works of Sôseki and his disciples were vaguely defined Neo-idealistic as against those of the Aesthetic (Neo-Romantic) School, while the group of writers who aggressively pushed an idealistic movement of the same nature as the Neo-Idealistic school but with more youthful and concentrated power, was the Shirakaba school. The name was taken from the coterie magazine, *Shirakaba* (White Birches) started by Mushanokôji Saneatsu, Shiga Naoya and several other graduates of the Peer's school, all sons of the aristocracy, while they were students at Tokyo University, for the movement grew, with this magazine as its base of operations. Because of the favourable environment in which they had been brought up, they could foster doubts about life and retain a vital sense of justice, ready to get indignant at the irrationalities of society. The proneness of the privileged classes to feel discontented with the existing state of society and themselves, imbued with radical thoughts from the very "ease of living and freedom of thinking" is a frequent phenomenon in many countries. It sometimes goes so far as to take the tragic shape of sacrificing the conscience of the time as is well illustrated by the examples of the dekabrists and narodniks of Russia.

The Shirakaba school deeply influenced by Tolstoy, had such a tendency especially in its early period; the behaviour of Arishima Takeo in his later years is considered to have represented this phase of the group. Mushanokôji's "New Village" was started also as a sort of social movement, and Shiga's writings reveal that he had an interest in and sympathy with socialism in his younger days.

In the last analysis, these sons of the privileged classes harbored radical thoughts resisting the old order of social values and hoping to create new social values as was convincing to them through their own experience, centered around their ego. They (as well as the novelists of the aesthetic school) were exactly the same as the young writers of the Taishô period who were to come immediately after them, in the respect that they all had confidence in regarding the newness of their own generation as a synonym for "rightness" and believed themselves qualified to criticize all things with their own intellect and emotion. They were children of a new age nourished by Chogyû's introduction of Nietzsche and the *tanka (waka)* of the Myôjô school. To those writers who had struggled through the ground-breaking period of Meiji, the assertion of the ego was invariably accompanied by an effort to expel inward resistance, but to these sons of the priviledge classes, it was a perfectly natural thing, the deserved right and pleasure of young men.

In the works of Ôgai, Sôseki, and Ueda Bin, the fathers of the new literature of the time, we often come across words of envy somewhat mixed with ridicule and contempt about their "newness." The disparity of generation between these guardian dieties of the new literature and their younger colleagues is quite evident in how differently they took the self-immolation of General Nogi. In Ôgai's case, it was not only the incentive to his starting the production of historical novels, but also an event to mark a turning point in his way of thinking. Also, as we all know, Sôseki expressed the shock he received from this event by such expressions as "following the spirit of Meiji to the grave" under the guise of the deep emotion of the hero of his *Kokoro*. However, to Mushanokôji and Shiga who had learned under Nogi when he was the Rector of the Peer's School, this "military officer of supreme loyalty" was only an object of their disdain and insubordination; even his death had no power to change their estimation of him. Mushanokôji once wrote, "When you compare General Nogi with Rodin, which do you think has more contact with the innate ethical nature of man? Do you think General Nogi's following the Emperor to the grave has the possibility of awakening the innate ethical nature of Westerners? . . . The suicide of Van Gogh on the other hand is much more human. It has the possibility of arousing the sympathy of enlightened people of every country."

Incidently, it is well known that Akutagawa wrote a short story, *Shôgun* (The General), also treating this subject.

To measure all things, animate and inanimate, only with one's own sensibility is to form all one's judgements according to one's own tastes as a criteria. A typical example of this is Shiga Naoya who makes his likes and dislikes the standards for judging good and evil. The individualism and humanism that they advocated were actually their own feeling about these schools. Though it was quick to mature, their art soon stopped growing, reflecting this lack of a theoretical basis. They at came entirely to turn their backs on society in proportion as the Japanese race became involved, at first in ideology but later in reality of the "modernity which had grown more and more common among the peoples of the world since the beginning of the Shôwa period, especially after the end of the First World War.

The writers of the Shirakaba school represented both such strength and weakness of the novelists of the Taishô period in general. The characteristic features which made them representative were a carefree and frank egoism coming from their good breeding enabling them to utilize such strength and weakness quite positively, staking their own lives on realizing their aesthetic view of the world as their ethics for life.

In this sense, the representative writer of the Shirakaba school is Mushanokôji Saneatsu. The combination of their self-admiration and the tradition of the 'I' novel characterized by the display of the self is considered to be the cause of the rapid advance and maturity of the literature of this school from the days of naturalism.

It was 1910 that the magazine *Shirakaba* was started by Mushanokôji Saneatsu, Shiga Naoya, Kinoshita Rigen, Arishima Takeo, Arishima Ikuma, Satomi Ton, Sonoike Kin'yuki, Kojima Kikuo, Yanagi Muneyoshi, Kôri Torahiko and some others. Unlike the members on the staff of *Shin Shichô* edited by Tanizaki, this group of young men were still quite unknown at that time, neglected and rejected by the literary world. Though some of the established writers ridiculed them, they all acquired undisputed positions as writers within a matter of several years. Mushanokôji soon grew popular with the public by bringing out the representative works of his early period such as *Omedetaki Hito* (The Good-Natured Man) and *Sekenshirazu* (The Puerile Person) in book form in 1911 and 1912 respectively. Shiga published *Ôtsu Junkichi* in the magazine *Chûô Kôron* in 1912 and Satomi Ton who was younger than the rest of the group published *Osoi Hatsukoi* (Late Virgin Love) in the same magazine.

The young men of those days, already tired of the narrow-minded, gloomy manner of naturalism, responded to these writers' youthful passions unstained with the filth of life. Sôseki, for whom they entertained deep respect, was sympathetic in opening the literary section of the *Tokyo Asahi Shimbun* for their contributions. There were some reasons for their early success, but the fundamental reason is their taking over the method of the 'I' novel invented by naturalistic writers and perfecting it. All the above-mentioned representative works written in the early stages of the careers of the three writers take the form of confessions of their private lives. While the naturalists employed their ideas of self as a tool to destroy established concepts of morality and old authority, the members of the Shirakaba school, who also rejected such old order and authority, regarded them as already having lost their power and value; the Shirakaba school made it their mission to rehabilitate themselves from the resultant blankness and desolation of naturalism. What they wrote were moral-culture novels or exhibitions of their own efforts for self-improvement. In this way, there was a positive significance in the 'I' novel as a form of literature.

Mushanokôji wrote in his *Tegamikara* (From My Letters) published in the December 1911 issue of *Shirakaba*:

"I saw paintings by Cézanne, Gauguin, Van Gogh and Matisse at Y's yesterday . . . and was excited. I thought an artist ought to come to this stage. I thought I was lingering halfway. Coming back home, I scribbled the following note: 'A heart wants to embrace another heart. But man fears it for the sake of his own existence. He conceals where his heart is. He believes such an attitude is necessary to maintain his position in society. Thus every heart feels lonely. Recent art seems to be trying to satisfy this yearning. I feel that recent art is the exposing of one's heart boldly on paper, waiting for another heart to come to it to embrace it. I feel especially so when I see recent paintings. . . . When I see recent paintings I realize the hearts of the artists touch my heart and I feel great joy. Art cannot be measured by old standards, nor can it be measured by new standards. It is the heart of man itself. I feel that new art is trying to touch the hearts of others by all means."

No one had ever expressed the idea of the 'I' novel, the ideal novel of the Taishô era, in words of such a beautiful and positive belief before. If you do not find this quotation satisfactory, read *Jibun no Fude de Suru Shigoto* (The Work I do with My Pen), *Jinrui Kara Deru Jiyôbun* (The Nutriment that comes from Mankind) and *Rokugô Zakkan*, all of which are in *Wakaki Hino Shisaku* (Speculation in my Youthful Days) compiled by Honda Shûgo. No other words show more clearly what meanings the 'I' novel had to the writer himself at the period when it was full of life.

Even from the above-quoted passage alone, it is clear enough that the inspiration Mushanokôji drew from Cézanne, Van Gogh and other artists affected him deeply becoming the fundamental idea of the 'I' novel. Mushanokôji writes, "Compared with bygone art, the new art is extremely serious, tense and deep."

The ideal of the 'I' novel of the Taishô period was to have literary works come into as close touch as possible with the "hearts" of the readers as the author's "heart" itself by discarding the fictional elements and "exposing his heart straightforwardly" in them. But what is still more important is that, at least, when the novel was just struggling to be recognized, such a practise was not of a "traditional" or local character, but appeared to the writers to be the surest short-cut to the "new art" of the world.

The doctrine of the 'I' novel had a similarity in its confusion between reality and truth to a distortedly imported scientism, but its perfection and its artistic theory were based on the desire to overtake the "new art" of the world. However reckless *Omedetaki Hito* and *Sekenshirazu* may appear today, we must not forget that they were attempts to stand abreast with the "extremely serious, tense and deep art" of Cézanne and Van Gogh. This was not only the character of Mushanokôji or even of the Shirakaba school as a whole, but also a character common to all novelists of the Taishô period.

Together with Kume Masao, they believe:

"To sum up, all arts have their basis on 'self.' If that is the case, the frank expression of the 'self' without a pretext for expressing other things, that is, the 'I' novel in the domain of prose art, must be undoubtedly the main road, the foundation and the essence of art." (*Watakushi Shôsetsu to Shinkyô Shôsetsu* or The 'I' Novel and The Inner Life Novel). In this conviction they had the self-confidence that they were keeping in step with the world's 'recent art.'

In this way, the influence of Mushanokôji was exerted on the whole of Taishô literature even with regard to the idea of the 'I' novel alone, and we may safely say that at least one of its most important moods was created by him.

"Mr. Mushanokôji has opened a new skylight for the literary world," wrote Akutagawa Ryûnosuke, while Satô Haruo further said:

"I believe what comes immediately after the naturalistic movement is the activity of the Shirakaba group. I mean those who have led us to the next period out of the naturalistic world which has already come to a standstill are . . . the members of the Shirakaba group, especially Mr. Mushanokôji. . . . In the world of art, nobody else but Mr. Mushanokôji has actually realized the aspect of individuality and the domination of the subjective, and other people have come to follow suit. I believe the emergence of Mr. Mushanokôji is to the present-day Japanese literary circles what that of Rousseau to the history of modern thought was."

These words of the contemporary writer are considered to be all the more trustworthy because he is a man unrelated to the Shirakaba school.

In this respect, Mushanokôji may be said to be the successor of Futabatei, for Shôyô had once called him 'the Rousseau of Japan.' In other words, the modernization of the Japanese novel was done by the appearance of several small Rousseaus, instead of one great Rousseau, cumulatively and in contradictory directions.

If some writer, who combined both the mutually opposing characters

of Futabatei and Mushanokôji and the characters they had in common
with Rousseau, had emerged, the Japanese modern novel would have
been different from what it is now.

But history did not take such a course. The fifteen years from the publication of *Tegamikara* in 1911 to that of *Watakushi Shôsetsu to Shinkyô
Shôsetsu* of Kume in 1925 was a period in which the 'I' novel formed
the ideal of 'prose art,' and this golden age of the literature of the literary circles ended when Mushanokôji compared General Nogi with
Rodin from the viewpoint of 'mankind.'

At first, the Shirakaba school's works were accepted only by the young
men and some observant people, while they remained the laughing
stock of older writers and critics including Ikuta Chôkô, but from
around 1914 or 1915, they began to write for first-rate magazines,
greatly strengthening their authority until at last during the middle
part of the Taishô era (1912–1926), they had become so influential that
this period might be called the Shirakaba period. *Washi mo Shiranai* (I
Don't Know Either, 1914 *Chûô Kôron*), which first popularized Mushanokôji (born in 1885 in Tokyo), and other excellent works published in
succession as *Sono Imôto* (That Sister, 1915), *Kôfukumono* (The Happy
One, 1919) and *Yûjô* (Friendship, 1919) were influential in making this
the Shirakaba period.

Partly due to the influence of Tolstoy from youth, Mushanokôji could
not be satisfied only with artistic success. When he was at the pinnacle
of fame, he purchased land in Hyûga, Kyûshû and made his "New
Village" there with the intention of creating the prototype of an ideal
community in which all the inhabitants could live as "brothers." This
plan was put into practise in 1919.

1919 was the year in which the First World War ended with the sur-
render of Germany, and the American president's declaration of democ-
racy and self-determination, along with the Russian revolution of the
preceding year foreshadowing the coming great change of the times, so
that Mushanokôji's movement caused great repercussions. His admirers
from all over the country came flocking to Hyûga, even disposing of
their family property in some cases. On the other hand, criticisms by a

number of social thinkers and economists about the fantastic nature of this plan were published in newspapers and magazines.

This project was a rare, interesting example of a Japanese modern novelist actually translating his social ideals into practise, though small in scale. Together with Arishima's giving away his farms in Hokkaidô to the tenants, it illustrates that the humanism of the Shirakaba school did not come from a hypocritical sense of justice.

Nevertheless, a utopian movement, carried out by a man who says, "I will make efforts for the sake of society and mankind only when what I do for the good of myself serves at the same time for the sake of society and mankind," cannot possibly succeed. It was not long before the movement was recognized as a failure by the public (though Mushano-kôji would not admit it and still preserves the remains of this community now without its theoretical meaning). This failure was the first step in the forfeiture of the spiritual authority of the Shirakaba group over the intellectuals of those days, and also resulted in a loss of self-confidence by the writers of the Taishô period in matters of social affairs. This is regarded as one of the causes for their increasing tendency to retire into their shells with the rise of the movement of proletarian literature from the end of Taishô to the beginning of Shôwa.

Mushanokôji was also cast into a nadir of discouragement at the beginning of the Shôwa period and did not rally until the ebb of proletarian literature. Generally speaking, his popularity as a writer has been quite erratic. As he had worked positively with the national policy during the Pacific War, he was purged after the war ended. After a period of silence, he wrote *Shinri Sensei* (Professor Truth) in 1950. Since then, he has been actively continuing his work with a harmony and composure never seen before in his work in the prewar days.

Mushanokôji believed the essence of art is "to have a heart that dances together with nature and mankind," however, his actions were liable to become exaggerated, conspicuous and somewhat hollow though attractive. Shiga Naoya who had the same thoughts on a narrower, but more solid track, consistently produced, on the contrary, very good works of art.

Born at Ishinomaki in Miyagi Prefecture in 1883, he came up to Tokyo while very young. After graduating from the Peers' School he studied in the literature department of Tokyo University and left without completing the course. With the launching of *Shirakaba* he wrote fine short stories and medium-length novels without cease for the next three or four years and gained the recognition of the public. The writings of this period include *Abashiri-made* (As Far As Abashiri), *Aru Asa* (One Morning), *Araginu, Kamisori* (Razor), *Rôjin* (The Old Man), *Ôtsu Junkichi, Kurôdiasu no Nikki* (The Diary of Claudius), *Seibei to Hyôtan* (Seibei and Guords) and *Dekigoto* (The Occurrence).

At the end of 1913 he was commissioned by Sôseki to write a novel for *Tokyo Asahi Shimbun* and left Tokyo to write it in the country. He began to write *Tokitô Kensaku* but could not complete it then. This was later rewritten and completed under the title, *An'ya Kôro* (The Path in the Dark Night). A bitter experience at that time became one of the motives for his subsequent silence from 1914 to 1917, during which period he lived at Matsue, Kyôto, Akagi and Abiko respectively.

His grandmother dearly loved him, but his mother died when he was still a boy. He was not much attached to his father, and to make matters worse, there was antagonism between them about their ways of thinking. Consequently, the discord between father and son grew into the keynote of his family life in his youthful days and became also the important theme of his novel-writing. All his medium-length novels including *Ôtsu Junkichi* (1912), *Wakai* (Reconciliation, 1917) and *Aru Otoko • Sono Ane no Shi* (A Man and His Elder Sister's Death, 1920) are of this theme, and in *An'ya Kôro,* it is used as a background of great significance.

Since early in life he was emotionally affected only by members of his family. He could only remain calm by having little feeling for others especially for those who showed no concern for the world which he had built from his own tastes and moods for himself.

He attained perfection through narrowing his world. Unable to get accustomed to the frivolity of urban life because of a too-delicate sensitivity, he rejected the snobs and their world finding his home among the unsophisticated villagers of Onomichi and Abiko. He created a unique literature which, it is no exaggeration to say, dealt only with his emotions about his family and nature. His dissatisfaction with the exist- ing conditions of Japanese culture and his feeling of alienation from society made him become religious. As a young man he was rather interested in Christianity and socialism, but these philosophies did not take root deeply, for he had to grope for the life he sought with all his own sincerity and sensitivity. In his representative novel, *An'ya Kôro*, the hero, Tokitô Kensaku is a purified embodiment of this pain for half of his life until he finds repose in unity with nature. This novel not only captured the imagination of many young men, but was also the object of admiration among contemporary men of letters. Among his other works, those short stories in which he describes his deep sympathy with nature, such as *Kinosaki Nite* (At Kinosaki, 1917), *Takibi* (The Bonfire, 1920), and *Yajima Ryûdô* (1925) are outstanding.

Other members of the Shirakaba school worth noticing are Arishima Takeo, Nagayo Yoshio, and Satomi Ton. Of these three, Arishima is the most important.

His talent and philosophy represent the literature of this school, and at the same time, stand well above it. Born in Tokyo in 1878, he was older than Mushanokôji and Shiga by several years. He had been a pro- fessor at Sapporo Agricultural College in Hokkaidô, after studying in America and Europe, before *Shirakaba* was first published. Thus, he had no personal contacts with the Shirakaba school at first. He became a member of the coterie perhaps through the introduction of his brother, Ikuma. He wrote highly individualistic novels like his maiden work, *Kankammushi* (Apprentice Shipwright, 1910) and *Aru Onna no Gurimpusu* (Glimpses of a Certain Woman, 1910–1913) which is considered to be the first part to his later work, *Aru Onna* (A Woman). Recognition of his talents came somewhat later than in the case of Mushanokôji and Shiga, because of his unconventional style utilizing Western sentence construction and consisting of a sticky, rather affected expression. He came to be well known after the publication of his elaborate works such as the drama, *Shi to Sono Zengo* (Death, and What Takes Place Before

PLATE I

NAGAI KAFÛ (1879–1959)

UDEKURABE (RIVALRY)

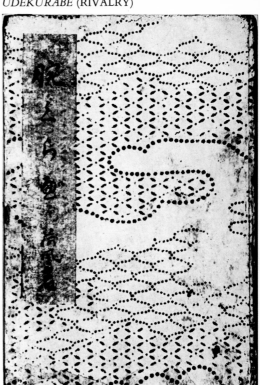

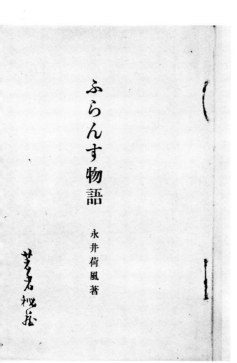

FURANSU MONOGATARI
(THE FRENCH STORIES)

ILLUSTRATION TO
FURANSU MONOGATARI

PLATE II

TANIZAKI JUN'ICHIRÔ
(1886–1965)

KINDAI JÔCHISHÛ
(TALES OF THE MODERN
LOVE FOOLERY)

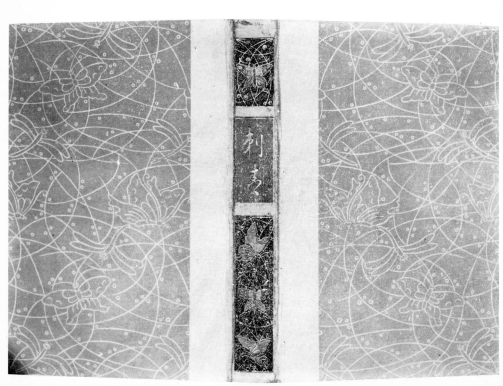

SHISEI (TATTOO)

PLATE III

MORI ÔGAI
(1862–1922)

OKITSU YAGOEMON NO ISHO
(THE SUICIDE NOTE OF OKITSU
YAGOEMON), PUBLISHED IN THE
MAGAZINE *CHÛÔ KÔRON*, JAN. 1912

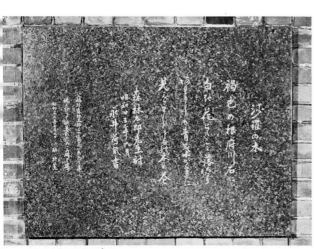

MONUMENT OF ÔGAI'S
POEM IN HONGÔ, TOKYO

THE MAGAZINE *SUBARU*,
THE INITIAL NUMBER,
JAN. 1909

PLATE IV

NATSUME SÔSEKI (1867–1916)

OUTSIDE OF HIS STUDY

PLATE V

WAGAHAI WA NEKO DE ARU (I AM A CAT)

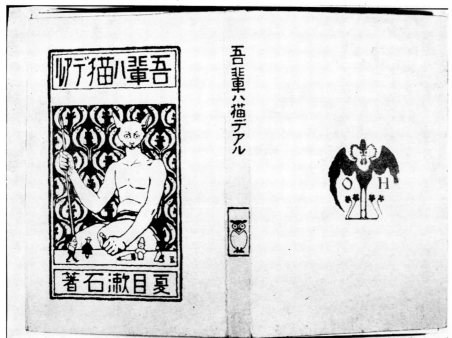

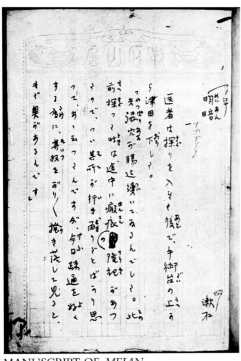

MANUSCRIPT OF *MEIAN*

MEIAN (LIGHT AND SHADE)

PLATE VI

SHIRAKABA GROUP, JAN. 1912
From the left of the front row: Tanaka Uson, Shiga
Naoya, Satomi Ton, Yanagi Muneyoshi, Sonoike
Kin'yuki, Miura Naosuke, Arishima Mibuma (Ikuma).
The rear row: Mushanokôji Saneatsu, Koizumi Magane,
Takamura Kôtarô, Kinoshita Rigen, Ôgimachi Kinkazu,
Nagayo Yoshio, Ôgimachi Saneyoshi.

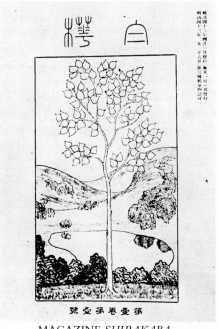

MAGAZINE *SHIRAKABA*,
THE INITIAL NUMBER, APR. 1910

PLATE VII

MUSHANOKÔJI SANEATSU (1885–)
PAINTED BY KISHIDA RYÛSEI

OMEDETAKI HITO
(THE GOOD-NATURED MAN)

YÛJÔ (FRIENDSHIP)

PLATE VIII

ARISHIMA TAKEO (1878–1923)

ARU ONNA (A WOMAN)

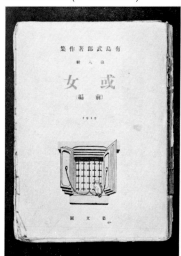

YORU NO HIKARI
(LIGHT IN THE NIGHT),
THE COLLECTION
OF THE SHORT STORIES.

SHIGA NAOYA (1883–)

PLATE IX

SATÔ HARUO (1892–1964)
A SELF-PORTRAIT

YAMERU SÔBI
(A SICK ROSE)

薔薇るめ病

短　篇　集

著夫春藤佐

MUROO SAISEI (1889–1962)

PLATE X

UNO KÔJI (1891–1961)

HIROTSU KAZUO (1891–)

KASAI ZENZÔ (1887–1928)

PLATE XI

KIKUCHI KAN (1888–1948)   KUME MASAO (1891–1952)   YAMAMOTO YÛZÔ (1887–)

A STAGE SCENE OF KIKUCHI'S DRAMA *CHICHI KAERU*
(FATHER COMES HOME)

PLATE XII

AKUTAGAWA RYÛNOSUKE (1892–1927)

RASHÔMON

MANUSCRIPT OF
HAGURUMA
(COGWHEEL)

AKUTAGAWA'S STUDY

and After) and the short story, *Kain no Matsuei* (Cain's Descendant) in 1917.

Next, he wrote colorful novels like *Umareizuru Nayami* (The Agony of Coming into Existence, 1918) and *Aru Onna* (1919) and essays like *Oshiminaku Ai wa Ubau* (Love Deprives, 1920). While he depicted the life of educated people around him, mainly females, he also described with full justice and sympathy the life of peasants, fishermen and working people of the lower classes, which hardly any other writers of the Shirakaba school had dealt with. His works with scenes laid in Hokkaidô in particular are very good. Such scope in writing about society shows his interest in all spheres of society. His mind, well trained by his solitude in America and Europe, had a far wider range than Shiga and Mushanokôji had, although their humanism, as well as for Arishima, was equally born of scepticism about the Christian faith. In this sense, he had much more in common, than generally believed, with Nagai Kafû who had a similar experience in America and Europe around the same period. When he was going to visit Europe, he said that he was interested in St. Francis of Assisi and Kropotkin most deeply. He was also an ardent admirer of Whitman, translating his *Leaves of Grass* and he is said to have had a great admiration for Brandes, Turgenev, Ibsen, and Tolstoy. This was the very process of the formation of his thought, which started from Christian benevolence as its basis and later turned to modern humanism, and then was further colored by anarchism. *Oshiminaku Ai wa Ubau* is an autobiography of his thought, and it bears the traces of an effort to escape from Christian influence and to systematize his own primary speculations on the basis of Bergsonism.

It was his theory that, if human life is divided in three stages, that is, habitual, intellectual and instinctive, true freedom exists in instinctive life. It has much in common with the theory of "satisfaction of instinct" advocated by Chogyû and is worth our attention as a serious attempt to give a generalized form of idea to the substance of the 'ego' commonly conceived by the writers of the Shirakaba school.

When young, Mushanokôji, Shiga and Satomi unanimously declared their respect for instinct. They were one with Arishima who said, "Thus, carnal knowledge obeys the will of Nature only when it is between mutually-loving man and woman in a state of dream-like ecstasy of joy." But it was Arishima alone who conceived the idea that man's true freedom is found in 'the height of mutual love or the healthy lovers' embrace' by committing love-suicide and ending his life at 45. His *Aru Onna* has been widely read as his representative work because the writer is dealing with a theme most suited for reflecting his unique philosophy. Since his youth he had been deeply interested in socialism and seems to have made a firmly-founded study of it, but it proved to be incompatible with his individualism. His social and financial standing was entirely different from that of the proletarian classes, and this fact came to torment him all the more as the socialistic movement raised its head in this country. He tried to square his life with his consciousness of socialism by releasing the farms he owned at Kaributo in Hokkaidô and portioning out the land for his tenants in 1922. Even such an endeavour, however, could not erase his consciousness of self-bankruptcy coming from the idea that the labor movement should be carried out by labor itself and that he of the ruling class could only appeal to the people not belonging to the proletariat to "shut their eyes with resignation" expressed in his *Sengen Hitotsu* (A Declaration) published in January of 1922. Along with his "love-for-love's sake" theory, it was a strong influence in hastening his death.

In short, Arishima was a man who could not help behaving like a self-conscious actor, on account of his broad mental vision and sensitive conscience. Subjectively, he was sincerity itself, but his writings and actions were always shadowed by Shirakabaesque moral-narcissism and elitism, and had an exaggerated Western style causing misunderstanding and antipathy. He lived single-mindedly enduring such mockery for his style, and represents through his colorful works, together with the life and works of Mushanokôji, the character of the Shirakaba school, and furthermore a phase of Taishô literature. It is of deep interest as a course taken by a pure soul, who, living in a period most favourable throughout the modern history of this country and blessed with the best possible environment and personal aptitude, felt these advantages to be a burden.

His death in this sense is an incident in the cultural history of Japan, and with Akutagawa who died a death of the similar nature he had a good reason to say, "The one who begot me will soon beget another I."

Satomi Ton (real name, Yamanouchi Hideo), born in Tokyo in 1888, is Arishima's youngest brother. He seems to have harbored a hatred against his brother's "pose," and in *Anjôke no Kyôdai* (The Brothers in the Anjô Family, 1931) he attacked him in an almost merciless manner.

He was more strongly influenced by Shiga than by his brother, and excelled in short stories. He first became well known by his *Osoi Hatsukoi* (Late Virgin Love, 1915), an autobiographical story describing the complicated circumstances of his own marriage. Then he published volume after volume of fine medium-length and short stories, such as *Zenshin Akushin* (Virtue and Vice, 1916), *Niwaka Are* (The Sudden Storm, same year), *Chichioya* (The Father) and *Ginjirô no Kataude* (Ginjirô's One Arm, 1917). Furthermore, he wrote long works including *Tajôbusshin* (Tender-heartedness, 1923) by which he broke new ground in the *demi-monde* novel in the wake of Kyôka and Kafû, rather than by the Shirakaba school.

Contrary to his brother who led a life comparable to that of a business man who failed because he had extended his activities too wide, he has consistently maintained the attitude of a conscientious artisan doing only 'what he knows well' and kept his position as a second-rate writer even up to now, surviving the vicissitudes of the times.

Nagayo Yoshio also published masterpieces like the novel *Mômoku no Kawa* (The Blind River, 1914), the play *Kôu to Ryûhô* (Hsiangyü and Liupang, 1916), the novel *Seidô no Kirisuto* (Christ in Bronze, 1922), and the long novel *Takezawa sensei to Iû Hito* (The Man Called Mr. Takezawa, 1924). For these works, he is highly placed as the writer to represent the masculine phase of the idealism of the Shirakaba group, but he lacks in some appeal to be a first rate novelist. This shortcoming is apparent in his postwar ambitious works *Yasei no Yûwaku* (The Temptation of The Wild, 1949) and *Sono Yo* (That Night, 1950–1951).

Besides those already mentioned above, Kurata Hyakuzô cannot be omitted here as a writer closely related to the group. He attracted public attention with his play *Shukke to Sono Deshi* (The Priest and His Diciple) in 1916, and has since become a writer representing the religious 'atmosphere' of the Shirakaba school by writing *Shunkan* and *Chichi no Shimpai* (The Father's Worries), although he was not a regular member of the group. His collection of essays *Ai to Ninshiki to no Shuppatsu* (The Start of Love and of Cognition, 1921) is a book widely read. With the very sentiment of the Taishô period, it quenches the religious or philosophical thirst such as commonly seen among young men of all times. In this sense, his writings may be said to be the religious literature representing the Taishô period.

CHAPTER XVI

The Intellectual School and the Life School

The greatest events in world history in the Taishô period are without doubt the First World War and the ensuing upheavals in all domains of politics, economy, and thought including the Russian and German revolutions. The war, which began in 1914 and ended in 1918, occupied nearly one-third of the entire Taishô period with Japan participating in it on the part of the Allies. However, the Japanese men of letters had surprisingly little interest in it. Even Nagai Kafû, who regarded France as his second fatherland, voiced nothing about it.

Such an attitude came more from complete ignorance of the meaning of the great events taking place, or their inability to feel the reality of the 20th-century war, than from their common inclination to retire from the world and indifference to social matters. Natsume Sôseki was usually a man of wide observation of such events: he had written a criticism about the Shinhai Revolution in China in his dairy. In 1916, however, about the First World War he only wrote:

"Of course, we cannot tell what influences the war will exercise on us until we actually see them, but at any rate we can scarcely expect any surprising changes from it. Since the war did not originate from any problems of religion or morality, or other things deep-seated in the hearts of humanity like cultural thought, sentiment, or aspiration, there is little prospect that whoever may win, the good will come to prosper, or that, whoever may lose, the truth will become powerless or that the beautiful will grow less bright on that account." (*Shin'eiroku*, The Record of True Aspects). These impressions are interesting today in pointing out the character of the First World War which had its roots in economic rivalry rather than ideological conflict, and at the same time it clearly reveals the disposition of the literary men of the Taishô period. Sôseki continues: "As a matter of fact, I do not think that this war will bring about any results which can revolutionize the faith of mankind. Nor can I expect that it will entail any large changes in conventional ethics. Much less do I fear that it will disturb the existing aesthetic standards. In no respect does it seem likely that the war will lead to a sudden change in our spiritual life or to an acute turn of the main stream of civilization."

Fortunately or unfortunately, Sôseki who died toward the end of that year did not see his prophecy entirely collapse. The Russian communist revolution broke out in November 1917, and the Great War came to an end with the fall of the German Imperial Regime in November 1918. Sôseki's prophecy, however, holds a different interest for us today. It shows how Japan was isolated from the world "spirit of the times." Without this kind of evidence, it is hard to imagine that the archipelago, Japan, could be so detached from the outside world just forty years ago.

The agitations and confusions of our generation's "spiritual life" which started between the late Taishô period and the early Shôwa period and are still continuing even after the Second World War, are similar to the struggles of those writers and thinkers, who lived in this remote archipelago, in their being drawn into a "modernity" common to the world.

If that is so, Sôseki's words corroborate that when its first wave washed the shore of Japan in the form of new thought in all domains of politics, religion, morality and aesthetics as 'revolutions in faith,' 'large changes in ethical conceptions' and 'disturbances of aesthetic standards' which took place in all countries of the world as unexpected consequences of the war, the Japanese literary men of the time were not at all prepared to receive it.

Perhaps here lies the reason why the early proletarian literary movement and Neo-sensualist movement, although they did not produce any works of great literary value, proved to be such a great menace to established writers.

Both proletarian literature under the influence of the Russian Revolution and the Neo-sensualist school, influenced from American-style urbane life were manifestations of the 'acute turn in the main current of civilization' which established writers had least expected. The postwar avant-garde art which became the pattern for such movements was enough to overthrow their views that the 'I' novel was the newest art of the world, simply in the sense that it was a product of the new age.

It was only while Japan as a whole was able to retain the position of a detachment in the spiritual life of the world that the idea of the 'I' novel conceived by the literary circle, a special island spiritually isolated from society, continued to exist as the ideal of novels beyond doubt.

Nevertheless, the several years' from 1915 or 1916 when the Aesthetic school and the Shirakaba group paved the way for Taishô literature to about 1923 when the Great Earthquake of the Kantô District took place was a spectacular one even in the whole Japanese literary history extending over one thousand years. Young talented writers emerged at an extraordinary rate in this short period as if to symbolize the flourishing of the short-lived modern Japan.

Most of them still active are now over 60 years of age, but nearly none of their works today are better than what was achieved in their youthful days. This is not because of the quality of their talents but is rather attributable to the fact that the harmony of various delicate conditions in those days has later been entirely lost.

Of those whom we may call purely Taishô period writers (unlike the members of the Aesthetic school and the Shirakaba group they began writing novels in that period), the chronologically earliest were a group of people who worked together to start the literary magazine *Kiseki* (Miracle) under the leadership of Hirotsu Kazuo, Kasai Zenzô and Tanizaki Seiji. Kasai wrote his first work *Kanashiki Chichi* (The Wretched Father) for *Kiseki* in 1912, and Hirotsu became recognized exclusively for his essays about the same time. But it was not until Hirotsu established a sort of neo-naturalistic manner with his first novel *Shinkeibyôjidai* (The Neurotic Age, 1918) and Kasai attracted public attention as a writer of unique 'I' novels with his *Nisemono* (The Counterfeit, 1918), and *Ko o Tsurete* (Together with the Child, 1919), that the works of these writers really came into the limelight. Soon afterward, Uno Kôji, another member of this group, came to be well known as a new writer of a similar character with his *Kura no Naka* (Storehouse of the Pawn-shop, 1920) and *Ku no Sekai* (The Hard World, 1920).

They were all graduates of Waseda University or their group members. Deeply influenced by naturalism, they consistently kept an attitude of closely clinging to commonplace everyday life and look straight into its gloomy phases, while the aesthetic school had pursued singularity and splendor, and the Shirakaba school had sought after ideals. Of course, they too were not free from the influences of the times, and especially the humanitarianism of the Shirakaba school was clearly noticeable in them as a Zeitgeist. Representative of the group was Hirotsu. A sense of social justice first displayed in his *Shinkeibyôjidai* gradually developed into a still keener and deeper one as he wrote his subsequent 'I' novels, such as *Morozaki Yuki* (Going to Morozaki, 1913), *Yamori* (Wall Lizards, 1914) and *Nami no Ue* (On the Waves, 1915), and in *Shijio Idaite* (With the Dead Child in His Arms, 1916) he presented a mentally abnormal person as a new type of hero, thus building up his position as a writer. The characteristics of Hirotsu's work consist in an attitude to gaze fixedly at the darkness of reality, pursue ideals and try not to lose confidence in man. He intended also to reflect the trends of the times in his novels and give them as much connection as possible with society.

Kasai Zenzô possessed perhaps the most striking individuality of all the members of this group. He lived a life unparalleled in the whole of the Taishô period, and his works recording facts of his life, almost as they were, gave birth to a group of unique 'I' novelists peculiar to this country. They were called "the ruined type." Among such unhappy minor writers of brilliant talent were Kamura Isota, Kajii Motojirô, Makino Shin'ichi, Dazai Osamu, and Tanaka Hidemitsu. They all had more or less connections with Kasai. In this sense, Kasai who was not a prolific writer and always troubled by poverty, can be said to have exerted a large influence, which he might not have been aware of, on this group for posterity. He was the ideal type or even the "ancestor god" of the 'I' novel in following the practice of novelizing crises of life and creating crises for novelization.

Born in Hirosaki City, Aomori Prefecture in 1887, he became a protégé of Tokuda Shûsei, joined the launching of *Kiseki,* won a reputation as a rising writer, led a life of abject poverty and heavy drinking at the Buddhist temple of Kenchôji in Kamakura and then lived in Hongô, and Setagaya in Tokyo, and died of consumption in 1928. Besides the novels already mentioned, *Shii no Wakaba* (Young Leaves of the Pasania, 1924) and *Kohan Shuki* (The Lake-side Note, 1924) are excellent, and should be regarded as prose poems rather than stories.

Uno Kôji's light humor in his early writings has something in common with Kasai's works, but Uno was not purely such a "ruined type" as he was an Osaka man characterized by strong vitality. Talented as a good story teller, he gradually attained to maturity in art while leading a life of continual crises. His activities were the longest among the writers of the group, writing many good works: *Ko o Kashiya* (Lender of Children), *Yamakoi* (Yearning for Mountains), and *Gunkan Kôshinkyoku* (The Warship March) from his early period, *Kareki no Aru Fûkei* (The Scenery with Dead Trees) and *Ko no Raireki* (The Child's Past Life) after he had recovered from a serious illness in the Shôwa period, and *Omoigawa* (The River of Love) and *Akutagawa Ryûnosuke,* an essay after the end of the war.

These writers were well received by the public because their manner of writing inherited from naturalism and redolent of everyday life produced a fresh impression on the readers who had already been dissatisfied with the feeling of some lack in the aesthetic or ethical idealism. At about the same time, the intellectual school led by Kikuchi, Akutagawa, Kume and Yamamoto grandly brought fresh air into the literary world of the day from another direction, but first we must mention Satô Haruo, Muroo Saisei, Kubota Mantarô and Minakami Takitarô who were very active, but did not belong to either of the above groups.

Satô Haruo, considered from the time of his appearance and his manner of writing, comes just between the Aesthetic school and the Intellectual school. He was born in Wakayama Prefecture in 1892 and entered

Keiô University with the intention of learning from Nagai Kafû. Active as a poet from an early age, he contributed rebellious, social poems as well as fine lyric poems to *Mita Bungaku* and *Subaru*. As he was unable to make a living, he moved into the country near Tokyo to live in seclusion. *Den'en no Yûutsu* (The Melancholy of the Country, 1919) is a novelized record of his life at that time and built his reputation. It is not only his greatest masterpiece, but one of the representative works of Taishô literature.

In *Den'en no Yûutsu*, the main character is a poet. His delicate sensitivity and sharp intelligence presented mostly in the form of self-reflection, and the flowing high-toned style combine to make this piece an unprecedentedly beautiful depiction of modern Japanese literature. This is a genre that had its roots in the Meiji period and was brought to blossom in this novel. After that, he published original and beautiful novels of a blend of sparks of intelligence with the expression of poetic sentiments such as *Shimon* (The Finger-print, 1918), *Okinu to Sono Kyôdai* (Okinu and Her Brothers, 1918), *Utsukushiki Machi* (The Beautiful Town, 1919) and *Tokai no Yûutsu* (The Melancholy of the City, 1922).

Thus he was counted among the most eminent writers of the day and influenced the young men of later generations in particular. After the death of his good rival, Akutagawa Ryûnosuke, however, he came to a dead end in his art. Although he published later such full-length novels as *Kôseiki* (An Account of Rebirth, 1928) and *Kamigami no Tawamure* (The Freak of the Gods, the same year), he was not able to open a new field. He was also an outstanding critic, and his *Taikutsu Tokuhon* (The Tiresome Book, 1925) and *Junichirô, Hito Oyobi Geijutsu* (Junichirô, The Man and His Art) are the best critical literature in the Taishô and early Shôwa periods.

Both Kubota Mantarô (born in 1889) and Minakami Takitarô (born in 1887) were graduates of Keiô University like Satô Haruo. As Kubota was recognized by his *Asagao* (The Morning Glories) in 1911 and Minakami by his *Yamanote no Ko* (Native Uptown Tokyo) in 1911, they were Satô's seniors in this profession. Kubota born at Asakusa, in downtown

Tokyo, and Minakami born at Azabu, in uptown Tokyo, wrote works reflecting the tones of their respective towns. Among the former's principal works are the short stories *Uragare* (Withering, 1917) *Sabishikereba* (As I am Sad, 1925), *Shundei* (The Mire in Spring, 1928) and *Shiseijin* (Simple Citizen, 1949) and the dramas *Kokoro Gokoro* (As One Pleases, 1924) and *Ôdera Gakkô* (The Ôdera School, 1927). They all portray the circles of downtown merchants, artists, actors, etc., creating a small but immovable world of their own with his minute observations of man and with his unique poetic feelings.

Kubota was also well known as a *haiku* poet, and in *Shiseijin* he built up a mature style which might be called *haiku* in prose.

On the other hand, Minakami, in a good sense, fully displayed the temperament of a well-bred youth of the more affluent sections of Tokyo in his numerous essays collected under the title of *Kaigara Tsuihô* (Ostracism). His representative novels include *Ôsaka* (1922) and *Ôsaka no Yado* (The Inn at Ôsaka, 1926). Besides these, he wrote such works as *Eikyô Zakki* (Miscellaneous Notes on the Capital of England, 1922) and *Yotsugi* (The Heir, 1935). Instead of becoming a professional novelist he remained an employee of a life insurance company and later served as its managing director. He was a well-rounded man of common sense on one hand and at the same time was very fastidious and had a strong sense of justice and passionate zeal as an idealist on the other. These two sides of his character were happily blended to produce matchless lyrical works when he described views and people he saw on his travels to Ôsaka and England.

Muroo Saisei, born in Kanazawa, Ishikawa Prefecture in 1889, was an isolated writer and had a career similar to Satô Haruo's. Like Satô he was first celebrated as a lyric poet and later turned to write the novel after he had published an autobiography *Yônen Jidai* (The Childhood Days) in 1919. Next he wrote *Sei ni Mezameru Koro* (The Awakening of Sex, 1919) which was his representative work about his boyhood. It is an autobiography to follow up his *Yônen Jidai,* describing the scenes and manners of his home town and his own sensual awakening as a boy, all harmoniously blended together. While *Den'en no Yûutsu* is a prose poem of youth, *Sei ni Mezameru Koro* is a matchless prose poem of boyhood.

After that he successively brought out original novels of his own based on poetic sentiments, but because their motifs were his own emotions rather than his observations of man, these works proved to be sometimes very good and sometimes rather poor. So even after he was 60 years of age his fame as a novelist tended to be erratic. For all that he went on writing and publishing novel after novel untiringly without losing zeal.

His masterpiece in the early part of the Shôwa period is *Ani Imôto* (Brother and Sister, 1934), and among his postwar works *Inochi* (Life, 1954) is outstanding. Near his death in 1962, people were surprised at his still vigorous productive power revealed in *Ware wa Utaedo Yabure Kabure* (Though I Sing I am Desperate).

Shin Shichô is a coterie magazine published chiefly by graduates of Tokyo University. Its publication has been interrupted several times. It was during its third and fourth series by such writers as Kume Masao, Akutagawa Ryûnosuke, Toyoshima Yoshio, Matsuoka Yuzuru, Kikuchi Kan and Yamamoto Yûzô that it sent out a host of prominent novelists at once to the world, leaving the term 'Shin Shichô school' in the history of Japanese literature.

In the publication of the third series of the magazine started in 1914, Kume and Toyoshima were mainly active. In a fourth revival of 1916, Akutagawa published the short story *Hana* (The Nose), which drew from Sôseki the highest praise. In the first issue, Kikuchi published the plays *Okujô no Kyôjin* (Madman on the Roof) and *Chichi Kaeru* (Father Comes Home) and the novels *Minagekyûjogyô* (Saving People Who Drown Themselves), *Edokko* (The Edoite) and *Miura Uemon no Saigo* (The Last of Miura Uemon). Kume and Yamamoto who had been already known to some extent gradually came to the forefront.

The writings of this group were characterized by the predominance of intellect over emotion. They did not run mad after their ideals or indulge in beauty but calmly faced up to reality and tried to point out contradictions. Such clear intelligence gave the readers some refreshing impressions after they had tasted the excess of emotions of the Shirakaba and Aesthetic schools.

Naturally, attitudes differed with individual writers: some had a resignation to the darkness of reality, and others tried to live with such darkness willingly and energetically or turned their attention to the irrationality of society and attempted to reform it. However, what underlay all these attitudes was individualistic rationalism which they came to hold, in a sense, through the influence of Sôseki's thought.

The earliest to rise in fame among them was Kume Masao, whose dramatic work *Gyûnyûya no Kyôdai* (Brothers of the Milkman) was staged at the Yûrakuza Theater in 1914. As he was born in Nagano Prefecture in 1891, he was only 23 years old at that time. He established his position as a novelist by publishing *Gakuseijidai* (The Student Days, 1918), a collection of short stories based on his student life, such as *Jukensei no Shuki* (Notes of the Prep Boy), *Ensho* (The Love Letter), *Senshu* (The Team Members) and Seppô (Preaching). In 1922, he became famous with his novel *Hasen* (Shipwreck) which portrayed his own experience of disappointment in love. He also succeeded in serializing novels in newspapers after he had written *Hotarugusa* (Hare's-ear, 1918), and continued to write popular novels from the last part of the Taishô period up to his death in 1952.

Yamamoto Yûzô, born in Tochigi Prefecture in 1887, published his maiden drama *Ana* (The Hole) in the magazine *Kabuki* in 1911. In this sense, he might be a senior to Kume, whose play was produced in 1914, but he did not become recognized as a playwright until his *Seimei no Kammuri* (The Crown of Life) written in 1920 and later represented on the stage by Inoue Masao and his troupe. Afterward he published plays like *Eijigoroshi* (Infanticide), *Sakazaki Dewanokami* and *Dôshino Hitobito* (The Comrades) and had them staged one after another, making himself a representative writer of the Shin Shichô school in the domain of drama. The themes of most of his dramatic works in those days centered round the conflict between human sincerity or goodwill and the cruel reality of society. As they are also excellent in their dramatic construction, the three works mentioned above have been repeatedly staged.

After 1926, he began to write mainly for newspapers. He published novels like *Ikitoshi Ikerumono* (All Living Things, 1926), *Nami* (The Waves, 1929) and *Onna no Isshô* (The Life of A Woman, 1933) in the *Asahi Shimbun*, and succeeded in raising the newspaper novel from mere reading for amusement to popular literature having philosophical significance.

Kikuchi Kan, born in Kagawa Prefecture in 1888, on the other hand, devoted himself to developing the newspaper novel into recreational reading after he had attained success as a writer of newspaper novels with his *Shinju Fujin* (Madam Pearl) in 1920. Perhaps for this reason his full-length novels which won him a reputation in the latter half of his life, including *Niitama* (New Jewel) and *Shôhai* (Victory and Defeat), have now entirely lost their readers. Among the works in the first half of his life, however, there are diversified works of clear intellect unique in Japan.

His autobiographical writing of adolescence like the short story, *Mumeisakka no Nikki* (Diary of an Unknown Writer, 1918), and his historical novels such as *Tadanaokyô Gyôjôki* (An Account of Lord Tadanao's Behaviour, 1918), *Onshû no Kanata ni* (The Realm Beyond, 1919) and *Rangaku Kotohajime* (The Beginning of Dutch Learning in Japan, 1921) as well as his early "theme literature" display the egoism of man through uniquely uncovering the realities of life with a scalpel of a keen and magnanimous psychological analysis, pointing out the absurdity of trying to cover these realities rather than facing their ugliness itself, implying that truly happy relations come from accepting reality as it is. Kikuchi and Yamamoto were successful not just because they were psychological analysts, but because they were able to develop the doctrine of egoism into a tool for analysis, making a sort of public morality.

Akutagawa Ryûnosuke (born in Tokyo in 1892) lived the doctrine shared by them in a more thoroughgoing aesthetic way and died a martyr to his own elegant taste. In this respect, he was a follower of Sôseki who regarded taste as the highest morality, and a successor to Shimamura Hôgetsu who believed that the only sincerity allowed to modern people was to admit the loss of morality. Akutagawa was convinced that "morality was another name for convenience" and that "conscience was too stern a taste." Thus it was quite natural for him to find his basis for living, in his art. In the Shin Shichô group, he was the only writer, inherently, of art for art's sake, a man who found his reason for living in the autonomy of art.

Most of the novelists in the Taishô era had such an attitude toward art, and in this respect, Shiga Naoya, Satô Haruo and Kasai Zenzô were more akin to Akutagawa than they appeared to be. More clearly conscious of attitude toward art and morality, Akutagawa built up his minutely calculated art on this very consciousness. His early works were a challenge to life with the brimming wit of a young man believing himself allowed into the world of the gods by his own intellect and power through his art. His early works like *Imogayu* (Yam Porridge, 1916) and *Hankechi* (The Handkerchief, 1916) and historical and modern-life short stories published under such titles as *Rashômon* (1917), *Tabako to Akuma* (Tobacco and the Devil, 1917), *Kairaishi* (The Puppet-Player, 1919) and *Kagedôrô* (The Revolving Lantern, 1920) are fresh, finely wrought works depicting the foolishness of man unconscious of his self-contradiction and the resulting humor, together with the author's feeling of superiority to them.

The liberation of his ego and the loss of morality which set him as one of the "gods" in his consciousness soon reduced his life to "hell." The struggle between life and art, which seems to have already been suggested in his *Jigokuhen* (Hell Screen, 1918) soon led him to write stories about the sordidness of life as analyzed by the intellect, such as *Genkaku Sambô* (Genkaku's House, 1927) and *Kappa* (1927) and ended in finally destroying the meaning of life in his works, making the author a tragic person who lost the meaning of art in life. In the hope of recovering the meaning of life, he wrote several desperate confessions like *Haguruma* (Cogwheels), *Tenkibo* (The Death Register) and *Aru Ahô no Isshô* (The Life of a Certain Fool), but he could not regain a meaning of life and committed suicide in February 1928.

Akutagawa's suicide seen from his own theory was an immolation of the flesh to the collapse of the world of art, his only spiritual abode. It was his last declaration of his intention to rule himself completely as a man always dealing with life and art with intense consciousness. His suicide was no less significant than the suicide of General Nogi whom he disliked, for it heralded the end of the Taishô period just as Nogi's suicide did that of the Meiji period.

The meaning of his death as the milestone at a turning point in Japanese culture has been already discussed by many people, but what is worth special attention from the standpoint of the history of the Japanese novel is that, as indicated in the dispute between him and Tanizaki shortly before the former's death, the collapse of his art was brought about by his having become unable to believe in "stories" or fictional structures of novels any longer. This is attributable to his lack of morality to serve as a basis for novel-writing.

As his opponent Tanizaki insisted in his *Jôzetsuroku* (The Voluble Note) and later practised, a novelist should have a system of values according to which he lives, or in other words, morality in the true sense of the term, if he wishes to give lifelike truth to the made-up thing called a novel.

Unfortunately, however, Tanizaki's morality existed only independently of the spirit of the times. Akutagawa, however, keenly felt the moves of the times in his way. Living himself in the moral blankness of the period, he believed that 'morality was another name for convenience' and said from the standpoint of a relativist: "If today's morality is an individualistic one, we may easily imagine that tomorrow's morality will be the opposite of this individualistic one. It will be an altruistic morality or a morality for the good of coexistence. No doubt it will be a morality which has as its object a certain social body consisting of many people." (Tomorrow's Morality)

As various aspects of the "acute turn of the main stream of civilization" taken by the world after the First World War came into focus and sociological change in Japan grew correspondingly faster, from the last part of the Taishô period to the early part of the Shôwa period, the spiritual emptiness from the lack of morality regarded as a form of sincerity, a condition continuing from the Meiji period, came to be unbearable to the intelligentsia as well as the literary men. Marxism, the "practical social science" was feverishly accepted by part of the educated class as a new morality to fill the spiritual emptiness. The Shôwa period, thus, began fraught with confusion and pain. Akutagawa having a premonition of these coming conditions more clearly than perhaps any of his contemporaries, chose suicide because of a "vague anxiety" about them.

INDEX PERSONARUM

Japanese Fiction in the Meiji Era (I.)
Japanese Fiction in the Taishô Era (II.)